SALSA
LOVERS
COOK BOOK

by

S. K. Bollin

GOLDEN
WEST ✴
PUBLISHERS

Printed in the United States of America

ISBN # 0-914846-80-9

Golden West Publishers
4113 N. Longview Ave.
Phoenix, AZ 85014, USA
(602) 265-4392

Contents

CHAPTER I
About Salsa

It is only reasonable that salsa is one of the world's favorite foods. What else is as versatile as this wonderful creation? Salsa is becoming a favorite in homes everywhere. For years salsa was referred to as that bowl of brightly colored vegetables, mainly tomatoes, onions and chiles, that one dipped a chip into. But no more! Salsa has come of age and the delightful common salsa has become a delectable addition to cuisine of all kinds. Salsa is easy to prepare and can create magic from the simplest of dishes.

Mexican food is the most popular and the most widely accepted of all ethnic foods. The foods of Mexico are colorful and exciting, easy to learn to prepare and within the reach of all food budgets. In addition, it is good for you and so varied that it is impossible to find it monotonous. The variety of uses of the simple tortilla are yet to be imagined! So too are the great salsas for which Mexican cooks are famous.

Mexican cuisine is as varied as the country itself but the love of great salsa is shared by all. Salsa is used with all types of dishes. Varieties are limited only by one's imagination. As cultures blended with time—Mexican, Indian, Spanish and others—each added their favorite tastes and uses. Originally, all salsas contained some form of chiles, fresh or dried.

Today's salsas are incredibly varied, not only in their ingredients, but also in their uses.

Chiles provide the basis of most salsas often combined with an endless variety of other flavors. Salsas that are red in color, from either tomatoes or red chiles, are called Salsa Roja. Salsas that are green are called Salsa Verde. Salsa Verde can be green because it is made from tomatillos or

because it contains large amounts of green chiles.

Both tomatoes and tomatillos require some preparation. If the salsa calls for peeled tomatoes dip the tomato into boiling water for about half a minute and remove with a slotted spoon. Run under cold water and slip off the skin. If cooking with a gas stove, pierce the tomato with a long fork and blister over the flame. Hold under cold water and peel off the skin.

To prepare tomatillos, rinse well under running water and remove the dry husks. Cut into pieces and simmer in water to cover for fifteen to twenty minutes. Let tomatillos cool before making salsa. Canned tomatillos are ready to use just as they are. One thirteen ounce can is equal to about three-quarters of a pound of fresh tomatillos.

To microwave tomatillos, remove the husks under warm running water. Arrange on dish or paper towels and micro-wave on full power for two to three minutes. Cool and use in salsa recipes.

While chiles are the principal ingredients of most salsas, creative chefs everywhere have made a salsa for just about everything. The ingredients of most salsas can be found in supermarkets all across the country. If fresh chiles are not available, dried or canned ones can be substituted.

Many salsas improve in flavor when they have been allowed to stand for a few hours. The exception is any salsa containing avocado. Adding lime juice helps, as does leaving the avocado pit in the salsa. However, the best thing to do is to add the avocado just before serving.

The uses and flavors of salsas are limited only by the imagination of the cook—so have fun, try new flavors and ingredients and enjoy the results. If you don't like cilantro, for example, leave it out and add chopped parsley or parsley flakes for color. If the thought of finding and roasting chiles is as appealing as washing windows, use canned ones. Remember, it's **your** salsa!

Common Spices and Herbs used in Salsas

ALLSPICE: Allspice got its name because its fragrance and flavor resemble a combination of several other spices, mainly cloves, nutmeg and cinnamon. Its most common use is in pastries, pickling spices, beef and ham and in sweet salsa.

BASIL: Basil is a versatile herb with a sweet, minty flavor that is especially good mixed with anything containing tomatoes.

BAY LEAVES: Bay Leaves, also known as Laurel, is used in cooked salsa, soups, stews and marinades. It is especially good with frijoles.

CILANTRO (Coriander): Cilantro is the leaf of the Coriander plant. The leaf, cilantro, is a popular flavoring and garnish for southwestern cuisine. Coriander seeds have a very different flavor than that of cilantro and are commonly used in stews, meat dishes and sausages. These are among the most widely used spices in the world and are one of the ingredients of curry powder. The coriander plant is grown worldwide and is also known as Chinese parsley. The dried form, whether powder or seeds, should be stored in the refrigerator.

CINNAMON: Cinnamon is used in both powdered and whole, or stick, form. It has a delicate, sweet taste and is a must with Mexican chocolate. It is one of the most popular spices and widely used in desserts, with fruits and with other sweets. The ground form should be stored in the refrigerator to retain its flavor.

CLOVES: Cloves are one of the world's most important commercial spices. It adds a wonderful sweet and spicy flavor and is used whole and powdered.

CUMIN (Comino): Cumin is native to the Mediterranean, as are many other herbs and spices used with chiles. It has been cultivated for thousands of years. Cumin gives a distinctive warm flavor to a tremendous range of foods, especially

vegetables and meats. In addition to its wide use in southwestern cuisine, it is also commonly used in Spanish and Chinese cooking and is frequently combined with cinnamon and saffron. Cumin should be stored in the refrigerator.

FENNEL: Fennel is available both ground and as seeds and has many varied uses. In Europe, fennel is a traditional seasoning for fish and sauerkraut. In the United States, fennel is used as a seasoning for pork, sausages and fish and as a flavoring for pickles. In southwestern cuisine, it is frequently used with vegetables.

GARLIC: Garlic and dried garlic are common in all salsas and other southwest foods except for dessert salsas. The dried version is a good substitute for fresh garlic and should be refrigerated to preserve its flavor.

GINGER: Ginger, an ancient spice, is found in several forms: ground, preserved, dried and fresh. Ginger is widely used in savory and sweet dishes and in oriental spice blends. Ginger is a major ingredient of curry powder and is frequently used with garlic.

NUTMEG & MACE: Nutmeg and Mace are the only spices that come from the same fruit. Nutmeg is the seed and Mace is the seed covering. They are widely used with vegetables, fruits, egg and cheese dishes and desserts. Nutmeg has a spicy sweet flavor and is used with Flan.

OREGANO: Oregano is an herb made from the dried leaves of a variety of the marjoram family. It is used in Mexican and in Mediterranean cuisine and is especially good with tomatoes, cheese, eggs and pork. It should be stored in the refrigerator.

PARSLEY: Parsley, both fresh and dried, is used universally as both a mild seasoning and as a garnish.

CHAPTER II

About Chiles

Despite what is commonly believed, the seeds of the chile are not hot. Chiles have a heat source that is very unique and powerful. This unique heat source is called CAPSAICIN and is produced by glands located at the union of the pod wall and the placenta. When the chile is handled, tiny drops of capsaicin are spread over the seeds and walls of the pod. This is why the mildest part of the pod is the farthest away from the stem end where the capsaicin is produced.

Capsaicin itself is a chemical compound that remains amazingly stable over time. It has no color, odor or flavor and withstands most conditions, including freezing and boiling.

As for rating the "hotness" of a specific chile—that depends on the taster. When a too-hot choice is made, holding milk in the mouth as well as drinking a glass of milk may help the memory fade faster. Adding one tablespoon of olive oil to a recipe with fresh, raw chiles also helps to soften the "bite."

For the more sensitive palate, in recipes calling for jalapeños, a milder green chile can be substituted.

Anatomy of the Chile

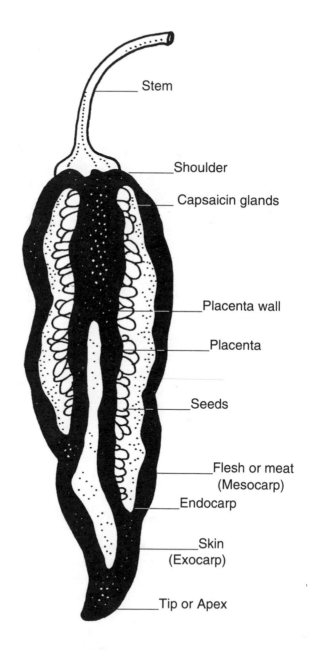

Stem

Shoulder

Capsaicin glands

Placenta wall

Placenta

Seeds

Flesh or meat
(Mesocarp)

Endocarp

Skin
(Exocarp)

Tip or Apex

A Cool Guide to Hot Chiles

When buying fresh chiles a few simple guidelines are:

The wider the shoulders (see diagram) and the blunter the tip, the milder the chile.

Generally, the smaller the chile the hotter it is.

Color is not related to fieriness. Red chiles are green ones that have ripened. The dark red/brown color increases as the chile dries.

Fiery chiles can be made less fiery by soaking them in warm salt water for a couple of hours.

Some Popular Chiles

The common large green chiles sold in most supermarkets are known as **Anaheim**, **California** or **New Mexican** chiles. Some definitions describe subtle differences between these varieties. Most of these chiles are mild. However, like all chiles, their growing location causes differences in heat levels.

When these chiles are dried, they are sometimes called pasilla chiles. These chiles are used to make chile strings known as Ristras.

The **JALAPEÑO** is perhaps the best known of all chiles. It is the small medium to dark green chile about 1 1/2 inches long that is common in supermarkets. It may be eaten fresh, roasted or pickled. When jalapeños are dried and smoked, they are called **Chipotles**.

The **SERRANO** is a small, bright green or red chile that

is the hottest of the chiles commonly sold in supermarkets. The serrano is especially good when pickled.

The **POBLANO** chile is commonly used for stuffing. This chile is always eaten cooked, never raw. It is a dark green chile about five inches long. The dried form is known as the **ANCHO** chile and is the most widely used dried chile in Mexico.

Chile names and identification can be confusing. In various states in Mexico, there are over two hundred different names for three botanically distinct chiles. No wonder regional dishes can be mysterious.

How to Roast Fresh Chiles

Roasting, or blistering, a chile involves heating the chile to enable the tough transparent skin to separate from the pod so that the skin can be removed.

Place chiles on a lightly oiled baking sheet in a very hot oven or under the broiler. The chiles will begin to "blister." If the chiles are not blistered all over, they will not peel correctly, so turn them frequently. When blistered, place the chiles in a paper bag for 15 minutes. If you are in a hurry, hold the blistered chiles under cool water to rinse off the skin. Which-

Blistering in oven or under broiler—Place chiles on a cookie tray or a pan, 3 to 6 inches below the broiler unit. Use high position of electric range or medium flame of gas range. Leave oven door open. turn pods frequently for even blistering.

ever method is chosen, wear rubber gloves to avoid painful burns to skin coming in contact with the capsaicin. If skin contact occurs, cover the burned area with vegetable oil immediately.

Unlike most burns that require cool water application, because the capsaicin is oil soluble and not water soluble, the vegetable oil provides the best relief. There are many other remedies for chile burns, but remembering to wear gloves eliminates the problem.

Chiles can also be blistered on stove top or barbeque grill—Place heavy wire mesh on surface unit. Use high position of electric range or medium flame of gas range. Turn chiles frequently for even blistering.

Or: place mesh over your outdoor grill.

For crisp, green chiles, remove blistered pods from pan or grill and plunge into ice water. For more thoroughly cooked chiles, place them in a pan and cover with damp towel to steam for 10 to 15 minutes.

To peel chiles, start at stem end, peel outer skin down.

Photographs reprinted from *Chili-Lover's Cook Book* by Golden West Publishers

Using Dried Red Chiles

All chiles begin as green chiles but as the fall arrives those that have not been harvested turn a bright red. Before the first frost, the red chiles are picked and strung into ristras, which are then hung up to dry, in the sun if possible. The red chiles are just as hot as the green ones.

To make chile powder, roast the dried chiles in a 350 degree oven for a few minutes, remove chiles, let cool and break them open. Remove the stems, seeds and any dark spots. Another method is to pour enough boiling water over the chiles to cover. Let cool on paper towels and remove stems, seeds and any dark spots. Grind the chile in the blender to a fine powder. Discard any unground particles. Store the powder in glass jars in the freezer.

There are many methods for making homemade powder, and a few cautions. Wear protective gloves, do not use a wooden chopping board and try not to inhale the chile powder.

CHAPTER III

Appetizers and Snacks

Appetizers in Mexico are called Aperitivos and may be very simple or miniature versions of such dishes as tacos, burros or chimichangas. One universal favorite is salsa, which is frequently eaten with corn tortilla chips. The fruits and vegetables that are so abundant today are also delicious when used for salsa dipping. Appetizers and snacks are foods for sociable times, to be shared and enjoyed with family and friends. What a wonderful way to begin a meal or just enjoy a snack!

All Canned Salsa

1 can (15 oz.) whole TOMATOES, drained
1 can (8 oz.) TOMATO SAUCE
1 can (4 oz.) diced GREEN CHILES, drained
1 Tbsp. dried crushed RED PEPPERS
2 cloves GARLIC, crushed
1 Tbsp. dried CILANTRO
1 tsp. RED WINE VINEGAR

Mix all together and store in refrigerator. This salsa stores very well and can be frozen.

Makes 3 cups.

All Purpose Salsa

4 cups TOMATOES, chopped
2 Tbsp. diced GREEN CHILES
1 1/2 tsp. LEMON JUICE
1 1/2 tsp. OIL (vegetable or olive)
1 tsp. DRIED OREGANO

Combine the ingredients and mix well. Let stand up to 2 hours to mix flavors.

Makes 1 1/2 cups.

*The smaller the chile and the more pointed
its tip, the hotter it is*

Aunt Mary's Salsa

4 med. TOMATOES, diced
1/3 cup SCALLIONS, chopped and including some
    green tops for color
1 Tbsp. JALAPEÑOS, diced, canned or fresh
Mix well.

Combine:
1 Tbsp. OLIVE OIL
2 tsp. LIME JUICE
1 tsp. OREGANO, dried (MEXICAN OREGANO,
    if available)
   Add to chopped mixture and blend well.
   Makes 2 cups.

Basic Basic Salsa

   This quick and simple salsa is easy to prepare and have
ready to dip into in a jiffy.

4 med. TOMATOES, chopped
1 can (4 oz.) diced GREEN CHILES, drained
1/4 cup ONION, chopped
1/4 cup fresh CILANTRO, chopped
1/8 tsp. SALT
   Combine in a medium bowl. This can be served chilled
or at room temperature.
   Makes 1 1/2 cups.

The larger the chili and the more blunt
its tip, the milder it is.

Basic Hot Salsa

3 med. TOMATOES, chopped fine
1 clove GARLIC, crushed
1/4 cup ONION, chopped
1/2 tsp. dried OREGANO, crushed
2 Tbsp. canned JALAPEÑOS, diced, or
     2 fresh JALAPEÑOS, diced

Dice tomatoes (drain if very watery), combine all other ingredients. Add the tomatoes, cover and refrigerate for a day or more for best flavor.

Makes 1 cup.

Bella Vista Ranch Salsa

4 med. TOMATOES, finely chopped
1 can (4 oz.) diced GREEN CHILES, drained
2 cloves GARLIC, crushed
1 Tbsp. OLIVE OIL
1 Tbsp. sweet cider VINEGAR
1/2 cup fresh CILANTRO, chopped

Salt to taste after all ingredients have been combined. This salsa is wonderful with everything.

Makes 2 cups.

Cherry Red Salsa

2 cartons CHERRY TOMATOES, cut into quarters
1 clove GARLIC, pressed
1 Tbsp. RED ONION, diced
1 1/2 Tbsp. WINE VINEGAR
2 Tbsp. JALAPEÑOS, canned or fresh, diced
2 Tbsp. LIME JUICE
1 Tbsp. SUGAR

Mix together all ingredients except the sugar. Slowly sprinkle half of the sugar and taste. If desired, add remaining sugar. This salsa should have a slightly sweet taste.

Makes 3 cups.

Crackers Salsa

6 ANCHOVY FILLETS, mashed
1 clove GARLIC, pressed
1 1/2 Tbsp. GREEN CHILES, diced
1/2 cup OLIVE OIL
3 Tbsp. PARSLEY, fresh or dried
LEMON JUICE to taste, not more than 3 Tbsp.
8 oz. CREAM CHEESE, softened

Mash anchovies, add garlic, chiles, oil, parsley and lemon juice. Add softened cream cheese and mix completely. Serve as a salsa spread with crackers.

Makes 1 1/2 cups.

Chiles are hotter at the stem end than at the tip.

Everyday Salsa

5 lg. TOMATOES, chopped
1/2 bunch CILANTRO, chopped
1/3 cup GREEN ONION, chopped
1 1/2 Tbsp. JALAPEÑOS, diced, canned
1 Tbsp. LIME JUICE
SALT and PEPPER to taste

Mix together and refrigerate. This is a wonderful snacking salsa.

Makes 3 cups.

Fast Fresh Salsa

2 med. TOMATOES, diced
1/3 cup ONION, diced
1 Tbsp. LIME JUICE
3 Tbsp. CILANTRO, diced
1 Tbsp. JALAPEÑOS, diced

Mix together, cover and refrigerate.

Makes one cup.

Packaged "chili powder" usually
contains other spices.
Look for "chile powder" which
is pure ground chiles.

Fresh Salsa

5 med. TOMATOES, chopped
1 BELL PEPPER, minced
1/2 cup ONION, minced
1 clove GARLIC, pressed
1/2 tsp. OREGANO, fresh, snipped
4 sm. GREEN CHILES, chopped fine with stems and
seeds removed.

Mix well and refrigerate at least 24 hours. If fresh oregano is not available, good quality dried oregano may be substituted, increasing the amount used to 1 teaspoon.

Makes 2 cups.

From the Can Salsa

1 lg. can (approximately 2 cups) TOMATOES
1 can (4 oz.) diced GREEN CHILES
1/2 tsp. GARLIC SALT
1/2 tsp. OREGANO
1/2 tsp. dried CILANTRO
1/4 tsp. CHILI POWDER

Mash tomatoes well, add can of undrained chiles. Stir in the spices and herbs, mixing well. Can be stored in refrigerator for several days.

Makes 2 1/2 cups.

Ristras, strings of red chiles, when hung by the front door, are believed to keep evil spirits away.

Instant Fire Salsa

Served over mini-tostadas, this salsa is a wonderful appetizer.

3 lg. TOMATOES, diced
3 JALAPEÑOS, seeded and diced
4 GREEN ONIONS, chopped
4 Tbsp. fresh CILANTRO, chopped

Mix together and let flavors blend overnight or for several hours. Spoon over tostadas.

Makes 1 1/2 cups.

Jane's Salsa

2 lbs. fresh TOMATOES, peeled and diced
8 sm. or 4 lg. GREEN ONIONS, chopped
1/8 tsp. SALT
1/4 tsp. GARLIC, pressed
1/2 tsp. LIME JUICE
1 cup fresh CILANTRO, chopped
1 Tbsp. GREEN CHILES, diced fine

This salsa is especially good when made with farm fresh tomatoes. Mix all together and chill.

Makes 3 cups.

The greatest number of wild chiles known in the world are found in South America.

Late Day Salsa

2 lg. TOMATOES, diced
1/4 cup ONION, diced
1/2 cup CUCUMBER, diced
1/2 cup CILANTRO, finely chopped
1 Tbsp. chopped JALAPEÑOS, fresh or canned
1 Tbsp. LIME or LEMON JUICE

Combine and serve at once. One zucchini squash may be used in place of the cucumber. A yellow crookneck squash adds a colorful touch.

Makes 1 cup.

Montrose Salsa

2 lbs. TOMATOES, peeled and chopped
6 GREEN ONIONS, diced
1/8 tsp. SALT
1/4 tsp. GARLIC, pressed
1/2 tsp. LIME JUICE
1 cup CILANTRO, chopped, without stems
4 Tbsp. GREEN CHILES, chopped

If avocados are in season, they are a very good addition to this all-purpose salsa. The lime juice helps keep the avocado fresh.

Makes 3 cups.

***Packaged, commercial chile powder
should be stored in the refrigerator.***

New England Salsa

4 med. TOMATOES, diced
1 sm. ONION, diced
1 BELL PEPPER, any color, diced
1 can (4 oz.) diced GREEN CHILES, drained
1/2 tsp. dried OREGANO
1/4 tsp. SALT
1/4 tsp. ground CUMIN (COMINO)
1/2 cup fresh CILANTRO, chopped, or
    1 Tbsp. dried CILANTRO
1 Tbsp. ORANGE JUICE

Mix together and chill 1 hour. This salsa suits the New Englander's taste for mildly hot and spicy foods.

Makes 2 cups.

Patagonia Salsa

1 can (8 oz.) TOMATO SAUCE
1 lg. can whole TOMATOES, drained and chopped
1 can (4 oz.) diced GREEN CHILES
1 Tbsp. dried CILANTRO
1 tsp. LEMON JUICE
1 tsp. dried and crushed RED CHILES
1/4 tsp. SUGAR

Mix well and refrigerate. Serve well chilled.

Makes 3 cups.

Green chile pods are considered a vegetable.

Quick and Easy Salsa

3 med. TOMATOES, diced
1 sm. GREEN CHILE, with seeds and stems removed,
    diced fine
1/4 cup ONION, diced
1/8 tsp. SALT

Combine and chill for 1 hour. This versatile salsa can be used for almost any dish. It is especially good with tacos.

Makes 1 cup.

Salsa for a Crowd

3 cans (28 oz.) stewed TOMATOES
1 can (15 oz.) TOMATO SAUCE
3 med. fresh TOMATOES, diced
3 bunches GREEN ONIONS, chopped
1 Tbsp. canned, chopped JALAPEÑOS
2 cloves GARLIC, pressed
1 bunch fresh CILANTRO, chopped
1 can (7 oz.) chopped GREEN CHILES
1 tsp. SUGAR

Mix well and store in glass jars in refrigerator for up to a week.

Makes 6 cups.

Red chile pods are considered a spice.

Tiger Salsa

4 med. TOMATOES, diced
1 JALAPEÑO, seeded and diced fine
1/4 cup ONION, diced
1/4 cup OLIVE OIL
2 Tbsp. LIME JUICE
1 Tbsp. THYME, dried
2 Tbsp. CILANTRO, dried

Mix all together and refrigerate for at least 1 day. This salsa keeps well for up to a week in the refrigerator.

Makes 2 cups.

Chile or chili? Chile is the Spanish spelling
and refers to the plant and pods.
Chili refers to a specific recipe such
as Chili con Carne.

CHAPTER IV

Main Dishes

These delicious and varied salsas usually accompany the main course, but their uses are truly unlimited. Salsa ingredients, especially chiles, are within everyone's reach—in supermarkets, in home gardens, both outdoors and in, even by mail order. Tomatoes, as well as most other ingredients, are available fresh, canned or dried, everywhere. Each salsa should be enjoyed in whatever way suits the chef!

Any Meat Salsa

1 can (4 oz.) diced GREEN CHILES
2 Tbsp. ALLSPICE
1 tsp. ground NUTMEG
1 tsp. ground CINNAMON
1/4 cup LIME JUICE

Bake or grill meat of choice (lamb chops are very good). Mash all ingredients together with fork and spoon over meat the last few minutes of cooking.

Makes 1 cup. Allow 1 tablespoon per serving.

Aunt Helen's Salsa Picante

1 BELL PEPPER, any color, seeded and chopped
1 med. ONION, chopped
2 stalks CELERY, cut into 3 inch lengths
1 can (8 oz.) TOMATO SAUCE
2 sm. YELLOW CHILES, seeded and diced

Cook all together, simmering for 15 minutes. Add water to cover the vegetables, if necessary. Cool to room temperature. Place in blender and blend until smooth. Reheat and serve as a poultry salsa.

Makes 1 1/2 cups.

Chiles now have their own monthly magazines, numerous books, festivals and fan clubs.

Avocado Salsa

2 lg. ripe AVOCADOS, peeled and mashed
1 8 oz. CREAM CHEESE, softened
3 Tbsp. LIME JUICE
1 can (7 oz.) diced GREEN CHILES

Combine and blend all the ingredients. Serve as a topping for cooked vegetables.

Makes 1 1/2 cups.

Avocado Salsa for Fish

1 lg. AVOCADO, mashed
1/4 cup ONION, finely minced
2 tsp. LIME JUICE
2 tsp. OLIVE OIL
1/4 tsp. TABASCO® sauce
2 tsp. dried CILANTRO or PARSLEY

Combine all ingredients well. Serve in small individual bowls at room temperature.

Makes 1 cup.

It's fun and easy to grow your own chiles.
They are perfect for container gardening
and many varieties of chile seeds are now sold in
garden centers as well as by mall.

Barbecue Salsa

This thick salsa is brushed on ribs while cooking.

1 cup MAYONNAISE
1 cup bottled CHILI SAUCE
2 Tbsp. WORCESTERSHIRE SAUCE
3 Tbsp. CRUSHED RED PEPPERS, from jar
GARLIC SALT to taste

Mix all ingredients together and brush on meat while cooking.

Makes 2 cups.

Basic Salsa Verde I

1/2 cup ONION, chopped
2 cloves GARLIC, pressed
2 Tbsp. OIL
1/2 tsp. CUMIN, ground
6 ANAHEIM CHILES, roasted, seeded and diced
1 1/2 cup WATER

Sauté onion and garlic in oil until onion becomes soft. Add cumin, water and chiles and simmer 20 minutes.

Makes 1 3/4 cups.

Anaheim chiles are also known as "California" chiles

Basic Salsa Verde II

1 3/4 cups canned TOMATILLOS, drained
1 clove GARLIC
2 JALAPEÑOS, roasted, peeled and seed removed
1/2 cup fresh CILANTRO, chopped

Place all ingredients in blender or food processor. Refrigerate several hours.

Makes 2 cups.

Black Bean Salsa

1 can (15 oz.) BLACK BEANS, drained
1 Tbsp. OIL, vegetable or olive
1/2 cup PIMENTOS, diced
1/8 tsp. ground CUMIN (COMINO)
1/2 cup fresh CILANTRO, chopped
4 GREEN ONIONS, diced
1 Tbsp. LIME JUICE

Mix together and refrigerate until well chilled. This salsa is especially good with chicken and pork.

Makes 2 1/2 cups.

Many types of chiles can be grown
successfully as houseplants.

Black Olive Salsa

This is the preferred salsa for tacos on southern Arizona ranches.

3 lbs. TOMATOES, chopped
1 1/2 cups BLACK OLIVES, sliced
1/4 cup ONION, diced
1/2 cup fresh CILANTRO, chopped
1 Tbsp. BASIL VINEGAR

Combine all ingredients and chill for several hours in refrigerator.

Makes 3 1/2 cups.

Blender Salsa Verde

1 lb. TOMATILLOS
1 Tbsp. JALAPEÑOS, canned
1 cup CHICKEN BROTH
1/4 cup fresh CILANTRO, chopped

Cook tomatillos as described in Chapter Three. Place all ingredients in blender and blend until finely pureed.

Makes 3 cups.

Chiles are one of the earliest plants
cultivated in the New World.

Bright Salsa

This colorful salsa adds a festive touch to meals. It is equally delicious served either hot or chilled.

4 TOMATOES, diced
1 can (4 oz.) diced GREEN CHILES or 2 fresh
    JALAPEÑOS, diced
1/2 GREEN BELL PEPPER, chopped
1/2 RED BELL PEPPER, chopped
1/2 YELLOW BELL PEPPER, chopped
1 Tbsp. SUGAR
1 Tbsp. OLIVE OIL
1 Tbsp. WINE VINEGAR
1 Tbsp. fresh CILANTRO, chopped
1 Tbsp. fresh PARSLEY, chopped

Combine all ingredients. Serve warm or chilled.

Makes 2 cups.

Cherry Tomato Salsa

1 carton CHERRY TOMATOES, quartered
1 can (4 oz.) diced GREEN CHILES
4 GREEN ONIONS, chopped
1/4 cup LIME JUICE
2 Tbsp. fresh CILANTRO, chopped

Combine all ingredients and chill well before serving.

Makes 2 1/2 cups.

***Salsa is a great emergency food which
can be made quickly from canned ingredients.***

Chile Cheese Salsa

1 pt. dry COTTAGE CHEESE
1/2 cup MAYONNAISE
1 can (7 oz.) diced GREEN CHILES
1/3 cup ONION, chopped
1 med. TOMATO, chopped
1 Tbsp. TABASCO® SAUCE

Place all ingredients and blend until smooth. Serve chilled for cold meats.

Makes 3 cups.

Chile Powder Salsa

2 Tbsp. VEGETABLE OIL
1/2 cup ONION, diced
2 cloves GARLIC, crushed
1 can (15 oz.) ITALIAN PLUM TOMATOES, drained, chopped
1/2 tsp. ground CUMIN
1/2 tsp. dried PARSLEY FLAKES
2 tsp. RED CHILE POWDER

Sauté onions and garlic in oil until golden brown. Add remaining ingredients and simmer 15 minutes.

Makes 2 cups.

In his search for black pepper, Columbus instead took chile seeds back to Europe. They were thus called "peppers" in the old world.

Chunky Salsa

This wonderful fresh salsa is not for the novice.

8 TOMATOES, chopped
1 sm. ONION, chopped
2 ANAHEIM CHILES, seeded, diced
2 JALAPEÑOS or SERRANO CHILES, seeded
    and diced
2 Tbsp. VEGETABLE OIL
2 Tbsp. VINEGAR
Sprinkle GARLIC SALT to taste
Fresh GROUND PEPPER to taste

Combine all ingredients and refrigerate until well chilled.

Makes 4 cups.

Cilantro Salsa

1 carton (8 oz.) SOUR CREAM
1/2 cup MAYONNAISE
1 cup fresh CILANTRO, fine minced
1/8 tsp. ONION SALT
1 can (4 oz.) diced GREEN CHILES
1 jar (3 oz.) PIMENTOS, diced

Blend all ingredients and chill well. Serve with chicken.

Makes 2 cups.

*The varieties of chiles grown around the world
are so numerous that they are
not yet all recorded.*

Coffee Shop Salsa

2 1/2 cups TOMATOES, unpeeled, coarsely chopped
2 cans (4 oz.) diced GREEN CHILES
3 Tbsp. fresh CILANTRO, chopped
1/3 cup ONION, chopped
1/4 tsp. SUGAR

Combine all ingredients and stir well. Let stand to blend flavors.

Quick and easy and found in bowls on coffee shop tables all over the southwest.

Makes 3 cups.

Cooked Salsa for Fish

2 TOMATOES, peeled and chopped
1/2 cup ONION, diced
2 cloves, GARLIC, crushed
1/2 BELL PEPPER, seeded and chopped
1 JALAPEÑO, seeded and chopped
2 tsp. LEMON JUICE
1 Tbsp. dried CILANTRO
2 Tbsp. OLIVE OIL

Combine all ingredients in blender and blend until almost smooth. Heat olive oil over medium heat, add blender mixture until bubbly. Serve over cooked fish.

Makes 1 cup.

Chiles are native to South America.

Corn Salsa

3 Tbsp. VEGETABLE OIL
3 Tbsp. FLOUR
1/4 cup BELL PEPPER, chopped
1 can (4 oz.) diced GREEN CHILES
1/4 tsp. DRY MUSTARD
1 1/2 cup TOMATO JUICE
1 can (15 oz.) whole kernel CORN, drained. Mexicorn (canned) makes a colorful salsa.

Heat oil, stir in flour and mix with whisk until all flour is absorbed. Add bell pepper, chiles and mustard along with tomato juice and simmer slowly until thickened slightly. Remove from heat, stir in corn.

Makes 2 1/2 cups.

Cucumber and Radish Salsa

2 cans (13 oz.) TOMATILLOS, drained and diced
1/4 cup ONION, diced
1 CUCUMBER, peeled and coarsely chopped
10 RADISHES, cut in quarters
1 SERRANO or JALAPEÑO CHILE, seeded and diced
1 can (4 oz.) diced GREEN CHILES

Combine all ingredients. Serve chilled with meats.

Makes 4 cups.

Archaeologists have traced chile cultivation in South America as early as 3500 B.C.

Day Before Salsa for Barbecue

1 cup GREEN PEAS, frozen
1 1/2 Tbsp. GARLIC VINEGAR
2 cups canned TOMATOES, drained and chopped
1/3 cup ONIONS, diced
1 can (4 oz.) diced GREEN CHILES
1/4 tsp. ground CUMIN
2 Tbsp. dried CILANTRO, crushed

Combine all ingredients, peas may be used frozen directly from the package. They will thaw in the salsa. Refrigerate overnight for best flavors. Serve as a side dish with barbecue.

Makes 3 cups.

Dry Salsa for Seasoning Steaks

This dry mixture is rubbed into steaks several hours before cooking.

2 cloves GARLIC, pressed
1 tsp. CHILE POWDER
1/2 tsp. LEMON PEPPER
1/2 tsp. ground CUMIN
1 tsp. dried CILANTRO, crushed

Combine all ingredients and rub well into steaks. Refrigerate 3 hours or longer before cooking steaks.

Makes enough for 6 1-pound steaks.

Easiest Salsa

A very basic and quick salsa when salsa craving becomes overpowering.

3 TOMATOES, diced
1/2 med. ONION, diced
1/ cup LIME JUICE
1/4 cup fresh CILANTRO, chopped

Combine all ingredients. Salt and pepper to taste. Best when chilled.

Makes 1 cup.

Easy Salsa for Pot Roast

1 carton SOUR CREAM
1 package SPAGHETTI SAUCE
SEASONING MIX, any brand
1 can (7 oz.) diced GREEN CHILES

Combine well and chill overnight to blend flavors. Serve with parsley sprinkled on top.

Makes 2 1/4 cups.

The common long green chiles known as "Anaheim" are also known as "New Mexican and Californian."

Easy Salsa Picante

2 cans (8 oz.) TOMATO SAUCE
4 cloves GARLIC, crushed
1 Tbsp. WHITE VINEGAR
1 tsp. ground CUMIN
1 sm. ONION
2 JALAPEÑOS, chopped
8 sm. CHILES, bottled in vinegar
1 tsp. SALT

Combine all ingredients in blender and blend until smooth and creamy. If thinner sauce is desired, thin with tomato juice or water. Serve warm.

Makes 2 1/2 cups.

Easy Salsa Roja

1/4 cup VEGETABLE OIL, not olive oil
1/3 cup FLOUR
2 3/4 cups WATER
1 package (1 oz.) dried RED CHILES, powdered

Heat oil, slowly sprinkle in flour, stirring constantly with whisk until all flour is absorbed. Slowly add water, stirring constantly until mixture is smooth and the consistency of gravy. Slowly sprinkle in chile powder, blending completely. Serve over enchiladas, burritos or grilled steak.

Makes 3 cups.

Freezer Special Salsa

5 lbs. TOMATOES, peeled and chopped
1 BELL PEPPER, seeded and diced
1 can (4 oz.) diced JALAPEÑOS
1/2 cup ONION, diced
1 cup dark BROWN SUGAR
1 cup CIDER VINEGAR
1 Tbsp. CINNAMON
1 tsp. CUMIN

Simmer tomatoes, bell pepper, jalapeños and onion for 1 hour. Add the remaining ingredients and simmer 30 more minutes. Cool slightly and puree in blender. Freeze in containers, thaw and heat in microwave.

Makes 5 cups.

Fresh Salsa I

2 cups TOMATOES, chopped
1 Tbsp. ONION, minced
1 Tbsp. OLIVE OIL
1 tsp. dried BASIL LEAVES
1 Tbsp. dried CILANTRO
2 JALAPEÑO or SERRANO CHILES, seeded and diced
1 Tbsp. LIME JUICE
1/2 tsp. dried ORANGE PEEL

Combine all ingredients and stir well. Let stand to blend flavors. Serve at room temperature.

Makes 2 cups.

Chiles are used dried, powdered, fresh ground, raw, cooked and any other way one can imagine.

Fresh Salsa II

3 lg. TOMATOES, chopped
1/3 cup ONION, chopped
2 Tbsp. JALAPEÑOS, diced
2 tsp. LIME JUICE
2 tsp. OLIVE OIL
1/2 tsp. dried OREGANO, crushed

Mix all ingredients well. Let stand at least 1 hour. Serve at room temperature.

Makes 2 cups.

Fresh Vegetable Salsa

This colorful salsa looks as good as it tastes.

4 TOMATOES, diced
1 ZUCCHINI SQUASH, uncooked, diced
1 YELLOW SQUASH, uncooked, diced
1 sm. jar diced PIMENTOS, drained
2 sm. JALAPEÑO or SERRANO CHILES, diced
2 Tbsp. OLIVE OIL
2 Tbsp. LIME JUICE
1/3 cup fresh CILANTRO, chopped

Combine all ingredients and mix well. Refrigerate, covered, overnight. Serve as a relish.

Makes 2 cups.

The genus CAPSICUM in the plant kingdom comes from the Latin word "CAPSA" which means box or box-like, so named because of the podlike fruit.

Frijole Salsa

1 can (10 1/2 oz.) FRIJOLES (beans)
3 Tbsp. ONION, minced
2 Tbsp. BUTTER
1 clove GARLIC, pressed
1 JALAPEÑO, diced
1/4 cup WINE or WATER

Combine frijoles and onions, sauté lightly in butter. Remove from heat, cool slightly and add remaining ingredients. This salsa is excellent with steak.

Makes 2 cups.

Garlic Salsa

In addition to being an excellent salsa for meats and fish, this salsa makes spinach flavored pasta a very special treat.

2/3 cups OLIVE OIL
4 cloves GARLIC, pressed
2 Tbsp. LIME JUICE
2 Tbsp. LEMON JUICE
1 tsp. dried OREGANO
1 tsp. dried CILANTRO

Combine all ingredients, and mix well. Serve at once.

Makes 1 cup.

For centuries dried members of the chile group
have been used medicinally as a gastric
stimulant and as a counterirritant.

Hamburger Salsa

4 cups TOMATOES, diced
1 can (7 oz.) diced GREEN CHILES
1/2 cup ONION
2 cloves GARLIC, crushed
1 1/4 cups CIDER VINEGAR
1/4 tsp. OREGANO, dried
1/8 tsp. ground CLOVES

Combine all ingredients and simmer for 15 minutes.

Makes 6 cups.

Herbed Salsa for Chicken

This is a salsa that is both cooked over the chicken and served as a table salsa.

3 Tbsp. OLIVE OIL
2 Tbsp. LEMON JUICE
1 tsp. ONION SALT
2 Tbsp. canned diced JALAPEÑO with 1 Tbsp. JUICE
from can
1 tsp. dried BASIL
1/4 tsp. ROSEMARY

Combine ingredients and mix well. May be brushed on chicken before baking. Serve remaining salsa warm as a table salsa.

Makes 1/2 cup.

Holiday Salsa

A traditional salsa for the holidays—especially good with turkey.

1 lb. bag fresh CRANBERRIES
1 lg. red APPLE (Delicious, if available)
1 lg. ORANGE, rind included
2 cups SUGAR
2 JALAPEÑOS, seeded and minced

Seed apple and orange and cut into chunks. Wash cranberries.

Place cranberries, apple and orange in food processor and chop together. Stir in sugar and jalapeno. Mix very well. Prepare at least 48 hours before serving. This salsa improves with age and freezes well. It makes welcome gifts.

Makes 3 cups.

Honey Salsa

This unusual salsa is popular in southwest Texas. It is usually served with grilled chicken.

4 Tbsp. VEGETABLE OIL
4 Tbsp. LIME JUICE
2 Tbsp. HONEY
3 lg. fresh TOMATOES, diced
1 JALAPEÑO or SERRANO CHILE, minced
1 Tbsp. fresh CILANTRO, chopped or
    2 tsp. dried CILANTRO

Blend all ingredients together.

Makes 1 1/4 cups.

Houseguest Salsa

1 can (15 oz.) TOMATO SAUCE
1 tsp. SUGAR
1/2 tsp. GARLIC SALT
1/2 tsp. dried OREGANO, crushed
1/2 cup WATER

Combine all ingredients, bring to a boil and simmer slowly for 1/2 hour.

This salsa is for guests who just can't handle anything hot but need a salsa for their tacos or as a dip.

Makes 2 cups.

Huachuca Salsa

4 lg. RED TOMATOES, unpeeled, diced
1 GREEN TOMATO, unpeeled, diced
8 GREEN ONIONS, with some tops, cut into
1/2 inch lengths
1 bunch fresh CORIANDER, chopped without stems
1 can (4 oz.) sliced JALAPEÑOS, drained
1/3 cup OLIVE OIL
2 tsp. LEMON or LIME JUICE
1/4 tsp. SUGAR
1 tsp. ground CUMIN
Sprinkle of GARLIC POWDER to taste

Combine and mix all ingredients well. This versatile salsa can be enjoyed with many dishes.

Makes 3 cups.

Salsa is a perfect food—high in fiber
and low in fat and calories.

In-A-Minute Salsa

Fast, easy and the ingredients can always be available in the pantry.

1 lb. canned TOMATOES, drained
1 can (4 oz.) diced GREEN CHILES
1 Tbsp. dried CILANTRO
2 Tbsp. white VINEGAR
1 tsp. white SUGAR

Combine all ingredients in blender. Blend until smooth.

Makes 4 cups.

Instant Enchilada Salsa

When a red salsa is needed for enchiladas, or perhaps tamales, this easy salsa does the job.

3 Tbsp. VEGETABLE OIL
3 Tbsp. FLOUR
1 jar (6 oz.) CHILI PASTE
WATER

Heat oil, gradually add flour, stirring constantly until all flour is absorbed, making a thin roux. Thin paste with water, beginning with 1 tablespoon of water, to consistency of gravy. Stir into flour mixture, stirring constantly with a whisk. Add water as needed for desired consistency. Serve hot.

Makes 2 cups.

Cilantro is also known as Coriander.

Lemon Garlic Salsa

This delicious and unusual salsa is served with lobster or shrimp.

1 cup BUTTER, softened
1 clove GARLIC, crushed
1 tsp. SEASONED SALT
1 tsp. SEASONED PEPPER
1 tsp. grated LEMON PEEL
2 Tbsp. fresh LEMON JUICE
1 Tbsp. liquid RED PEPPER SAUCE

Cream butter, add garlic, salt and pepper. Blend thoroughly. Add remaining ingredients and mix completely.

Makes 1 1/4 cups.

Lemon Salsa for Fish

A delightful cooked salsa served warm with fish.

1 Tbsp. CORNSTARCH
1/2 cup SUGAR
1/4 tsp. SALT
1 cup WATER
1 tsp. grated LEMON RIND
3 Tbsp. LEMON JUICE
2 Tbsp. BUTTER
1 can (4 oz.) diced GREEN CHILES, undrained

Mix cornstarch, sugar and salt in medium saucepan. Blend with 1/4 cup of the water until smooth. Add the remaining water. Stir constantly, bring to a boil and simmer until mixture thickens. Remove from heat, stir in the remaining ingredients and serve warm with fish.

Makes 1 1/2 cups.

Lime Salsa

2 lg. TOMATOES, diced
2 lg. TOMATILLOS, diced
1/3 cup RED ONION, diced
1/3 cup BELL PEPPER, any color, diced
2 Tbsp. fresh LIME JUICE
2 tsp. LIME PEEL, grated

Dice tomatoes, remove husks from tomatillos and dice. Mix together, add all other ingredients. Cover and refrigerate several hours or overnight.

Makes 2 cups.

Madera Salsa

3 Tbsp. VEGETABLE OIL
1 BELL PEPPER, chopped
1 lg. ONION, chopped
2 CARROTS, chopped
4 stalks CELERY, chopped
1 lg. can (28 oz.) TOMATOES with liquid
1 can (7 oz.) diced GREEN CHILES
1/4 tsp. SUGAR
2 tsp. RED CHILE POWDER
**   or 3 tsp. commercial CHILI POWDER**
1/4 tsp. ground CUMIN
1/2 tsp. dried CILANTRO

Sauté bell pepper, onion, carrots and celery in oil until bell peppers begin to blister. Slowly add all remaining ingredients, beginning with the tomatoes. Simmer slowly 1 hour.

Makes 4 cups.

Mango Salsa

1 MANGO, peeled and diced
2 Tbsp. canned JALAPEÑOS, diced
1/2 cup ONION, diced
1/4 cup LIME JUICE
1 Tbsp. dried CILANTRO
1/4 tsp. dried CUMIN

Combine all ingredients and refrigerate several hours. Serve with fish.

Makes 1 cup.

Mild Salsa for Beef

1/2 cup ONION, diced
1 clove GARLIC, pressed
1 Tbsp. OLIVE OIL or SPRAY
2 cans (8 oz.) TOMATO SAUCE
1 can (4 oz.) diced GREEN CHILES
1/4 tsp. ground CUMIN (COMINO)
1/4 tsp. dried OREGANO, crushed

Sauté onion and garlic gently in oil or with spray. Add remaining ingredients and simmer 10 minutes. Serve warm with beef.

Makes 2 cups.

Green tomatoes are sometimes known as tomatillos, but tomatillos are not related to the common red garden tomato.

Multi-Purpose Salsa

3 cups TOMATOES, diced
3 cups ANAHEIM, roasted and seeded, diced fine
1 cup CIDER VINEGAR
1 cup CILANTRO, diced

Combine and cook for 1 hour over medium heat. Remove from heat, let cool and stir in cilantro.

Makes 6 cups.

Not Hot Salsa

1 lb. TOMATOES, diced
1 can (4 oz.) diced GREEN CHILES
1/3 cup ONION, diced
1 Tbsp. dried CILANTRO
1 clove GARLIC, crushed
1/4 tsp. SALT

Combine all ingredients and let stand at least 1 hour. Serve at room temperature.

Makes 2 cups.

Most salsas can use canned, drained tomatoes as a substitute for fresh ones.

On-the-Top Salsa

2 TOMATOES, chopped
1 sm. CHILE of choice, seeded and diced
1/4 cup ONION, diced
1/4 cup CILANTRO, chopped

Combine all together and serve at room temperature.

Makes 1 cup.

Peach Salsa for Fowl

1 can (15 oz.) PEACHES, drained and diced
1/4 cup GREEN ONIONS, diced
1 Tbsp. LEMON JUICE
1 BELL PEPPER, any color, diced
2 tsp. MINT LEAVES, chopped
1 can (7 oz.) diced GREEN CHILES
1/4 tsp. ground GINGER

Mix well and refrigerate for 24 hours. As a holiday gift, use both red and green bell peppers. This salsa freezes well.

Makes 2 1/2 cups.

To peel or not to peel? In salsas using tomatoes
this is a matter of choice.

Pecan Salsa for Chicken

1 1/2 cups distilled or bottled WATER
1 cup light BROWN SUGAR
1 cup WHITE SUGAR
3 Tbsp. LIME JUICE
2 cups WHIPPING CREAM, unwhipped
1 can (4 oz.) diced GREEN CHILES
2 cups PECANS, chopped

Heat water, add both sugars and stir until dissolved. Increase heat and boil gently 5 minutes. Remove from heat, slowly stir in cream. Add remaining ingredients, stirring well. Serve as a gravy over chicken.

Makes 3 cups.

Pico de Gallo I

Use leftover Pico de Gallo mixed with cottage cheese for a lunch salad.

This marvelous salsa has become very popular. The recipes for Pico de Gallo are similar yet each has its own personality.

4 med. TOMATOES, chopped
6 GREEN ONIONS, chopped with some of
the green tops
2-3 JALAPEÑOS, seeded and chopped
1 1/2 Tbsp. VEGETABLE OIL
1/3 cup fresh CILANTRO, chopped

Blend all ingredients and stir well. Chill before serving.

Makes 2 cups.

Pico de Gallo II

Pico de Gallo means "rooster's beak" and, tradition says, comes from Veracruz. It has a distinctive texture and flavor and makes use of many different fresh fruits and vegetables.

1 1/2 cup WATERMELON, diced and seeded
1 cup JICAMA, peeled and diced
1 ORANGE, peeled and diced
1 JALAPEÑO, seeded and diced
3 Tbsp. fresh CILANTRO, chopped
1 Tbsp. LIME JUICE

Mix all ingredients. Serve chilled.

Makes 3 cups.

Pico de Gallo III

2 TOMATOES, diced
1/2 cup ONION, diced
6 RADISHES, diced
1/2 bunch CILANTRO, chopped
3 SERRANO CHILES, diced and seeded
1 Tbsp. LIME JUICE

Mix all ingredients. Serve chilled.

Makes 2 cups.

When handling chiles, if you do not wish to wear rubber gloves, coat your hands with cooking oil.

Pico de Gallo IV

3 med. TOMATOES, diced
1/2 cup ONION, diced
2 cloves GARLIC, pressed
1 Tbsp. canned JALAPEÑO, with 1/2 tsp. juice
    from can
1/2 cup fresh CILANTRO, chopped
2 Tbsp. BASIL VINEGAR
3 Tbsp. OIL (not olive oil)

Mix all ingredients well. Chill for 1 hour.

Makes 2 cups.

Pico de Gallo V

4 lg. TOMATOES, chopped
1/4 cup ONION, chopped
1/4 cup CUCUMBER, peeled and chopped
2 Tbsp. canned JALAPEÑO, diced
1 Tbsp. LIME JUICE
Sprinkle of GARLIC SALT
2 Tbsp. CILANTRO, fresh, chopped

Combine all ingredients. Serve well chilled.

Makes 2 1/2 cups.

Do not cut fresh chiles on a wooden or plastic cutting board as the oils are difficult to remove. Use a dinner plate.

Pineapple Salsa

1 can (15 oz.) TOMATOES, drained and chopped
1 sm. can crushed PINEAPPLE, drained
1 JALAPEÑO, seeded and diced
1 Tbsp. LIME JUICE
4 Tbsp. fresh CILANTRO, chopped
2 Tbsp. RED ONION, minced

Combine all ingredients and refrigerate uncovered until well chilled. Serve with zucchini fritters or with fish.

Makes 2 1/2 cups.

Pork Roast Salsa

1 sm. can PINEAPPLE RINGS, drained
2 Tbsp. RED BELL PEPPER, diced
3 GREEN ONIONS, sliced fine lengthwise
1/4 tsp. ground GINGER
1 oz. LEMON JUICE
1 oz. TEQUILA
1 Tbsp. fresh MINT LEAVES, chopped

Cut pineapple rings into 1/4 inch pieces. Mix with all other ingredients. Chill very well. Serve with pork roast.

Makes 1 1/2 cups.

*Do not cut chiles under running water
as the oils will rise toward your face
and can be very irritating.*

Quick Red Salsa

This is a quick salsa for prepared enchiladas.

3 Tbsp. VEGETABLE OIL
3 Tbsp. FLOUR
1 jar (6 oz.) RED CHILE PASTE

Heat oil. Stir in flour. Stir with wire whisk until all flour is absorbed. Stir in chile paste, thinning with warm water to make the desired consistency.

Makes 1 1/4 cups.

Rellenos Salsa

This slightly sweet flavored salsa is a tradition with Chile Rellenos.

2 Tbsp. VEGETABLE OIL
2 Tbsp. ONION, minced
1 can (8 oz.) STEWED TOMATOES
1 can (8 oz.) TOMATO SAUCE
1 CHICKEN BOUILLON CUBE
1/4 tsp. ground CUMIN
1/4 tsp. OREGANO flakes

Heat oil, sauté onions until limp. Add the remaining ingredients and simmer slowly for 30 minutes.

Makes 2 cups, enough for 6 rellenos.

A good rule of thumb—the smaller the chile,
the hotter it is.

Rincon Salsa

2 Tbsp. VEGETABLE OIL
1/2 cup ONIONS, chopped
2 cups TOMATOES, chopped
1 tsp. dried OREGANO
1 tsp. ground CUMIN
1 Tbsp. WORCESTERSHIRE SAUCE

Sauté onions in oil over medium heat. Stir in the remaining ingredients and simmer 5 more minutes.

Makes 1 cup.

Roja Salsa Gravy

4 Tbsp. VEGETABLE OIL
4 Tbsp. FLOUR
2 cups VEGETABLE CONSOMME
1/4 cup CHILE POWDER
2 cans (10 1/2 oz.) TOMATO PUREE
1 tsp. SUGAR
1/4 tsp. CUMIN

Heat oil, stir in flour with wire whisk. Slowly add consomme as in making gravy. When thickened, add puree, sugar and cumin. Simmer till thickened.

Makes 4 1/2 cups.

All chiles are green when new on the vine. As they ripen, they become yellow, orange and lastly various shades of red.

Salsa Caliente

1 lg. can TOMATOES, drained and diced
1/2 cup ONION, diced
1 clove GARLIC, crushed
1 Tbsp. ground RED CHILE POWDER
1 Tbsp. SUGAR
1/4 tsp. ground OREGANO
1/4 tsp. ground CUMIN

Combine all ingredients and chill several hours.

Makes 2 cups.

Salsa Carne

1 Tbsp. VEGETABLE OIL
1/3 cup ONION, diced
1 can (7 oz.) GREEN CHILES, chopped
1 Tbsp. canned sliced JALAPEÑO, optional
1 can (15 oz.) TOMATO SAUCE
2 cups cooked, drained GROUND BEEF

Sauté onions in oil. Add remaining ingredients, simmer 15 minutes. Serve over rice.

Makes 4 cups.

Dried jalapeños are called Chipotles.

Salsa con Tomatillo

4 TOMATILLOS, canned and drained
1/2 cup BELL PEPPER, seeded and diced
1/2 cup crushed PINEAPPLE, drained
3 Tbsp. ORANGE JUICE
1 Tbsp. LEMON JUICE
1/4 cup ONION, diced
1 tsp. JALAPEÑO, diced
1/3 cup fresh CILANTRO, chopped

Puree tomatillos in blender or food processor. Combine with other ingredients and refrigerate. Good with delicately flavored fish.

Makes 2 cups.

Salsa con Tomatoes and Tomatillos

3 med. TOMATOES, chopped
6 TOMATILLOS, husks removed, chopped
1 JALAPEÑO or SERRANO CHILE, seeded and diced
1 Tbsp. LIME JUICE
6 green ONIONS, cut in 1/2 inch pieces
1/2 bunch fresh CILANTRO, minced

Combine all ingredients and chill well.

Makes 2 cups.

Add a tablespoon of paprika to brighten cooked salsa.

Salsa Crema for Omelets

4 Tbsp. BUTTER
4 Tbsp. FLOUR
1 1/2 cup whole MILK or light CREAM
1/2 cup ONION, diced
1 can (7 oz.) diced GREEN CHILES
1 jar (3 oz.) PIMENTOS, diced
1 tsp. dried CILANTRO

Melt butter, stir in flour and blend with whisk until flour is absorbed. Gradually stir in milk or cream and stir until thickened. Stir in remaining ingredients. Serve hot, spooned over omelets.

Makes 2 cups.

Salsa Cruda

2 cans (15 oz.) whole TOMATOES, drained
    and chopped
1 tsp. JALAPEÑO, diced
2 tsp. LIME JUICE
1 tsp. OLIVE OIL
1/4 cup ONION, sliced very thin

Combine and let stand for 1 hour. This is an easy salsa for hamburgers.

Makes 2 cups.

**Add a few drops of red food coloring
to brighten uncooked salsa.**

Salsa for Baked Fish

1 Tbsp. VEGETABLE OIL
1 cup ONION, sliced
2 cups TOMATOES, chopped
1/2 can (2 oz.) diced GREEN CHILES
2 Tbsp. LEMON JUICE
1 tsp. CAPERS
1 jar (4 oz.) PIMENTOS, diced, drained

Heat oil over medium heat, sauté onions till translucent. Add the remaining ingredients and simmer 15 minutes.

Makes 3 cups.

Salsa for Barbecued Spareribs

This salsa is spread over ribs while baking or served separately at the table.

1/2 cup ONION, diced
1/4 cup LEMON JUICE
1/4 cup WINE VINEGAR
2 Tbsp. SOY SAUCE
1/4 cup BROWN SUGAR
1 can (4 oz.) PREPARED SALSA for tacos
1 can (4 oz.) diced GREEN CHILES

Combine all ingredients and cook to the boiling point. Reduce heat and simmer 15 minutes.

Makes 1 1/2 cups or enough salsa for 4 pounds of ribs.

Salsa for Broiled Fish

This salsa is brushed over fish fillets prior to broiling or baking.

1/2 cup MAYONNAISE
1 sm. JALAPEÑO, finely minced
1/8 tsp. LEMON PEPPER

Mix all well together. Salsa must be cooked and is not served separately.

Makes 1/2 cup or enough for 4 large size fillets.

Salsa for Chilled Shrimp

1 can (8 oz.) TOMATO SAUCE
1 tsp. creamed HORSERADISH
1 tsp. RED CHILE POWDER
2 Tbsp. LEMON JUICE
1/4 tsp. SUGAR

Combine the ingredients and serve very chilled as a salsa for cold shrimp.

Makes 1 1/4 cups.

When purchasing either cilantro or comino
in prepackaged form, store in the refrigerator
to preserve texture and flavor.

Salsa for Fried Chicken

2 lg. TOMATOES, peeled and chopped
1/2 cup V-8 JUICE
1/2 cup RED ONION, diced
2 Tbsp. canned JALAPEÑOS, drained or (4 oz.) can, diced GREEN CHILES

Combine and chill. Serve in small individual garnish bowls.

Makes 2 cups.

Salsa for Marinating Beef

Let beef marinate for at least 3 hours, preferably over-night, in refrigerator. This stores well in glass jars in the refrigerator.

1 cup OLIVE OIL
2 cloves GARLIC, pressed
1 tsp. dried OREGANO
1 tsp. dried CILANTRO
1/2 cup RED WINE
1 Tbsp. JALAPEÑO JUICE (from canned jalapenos)

Mix the ingredients together in a glass container and shake to mix well.

Makes 1 2/3 cups.

Cumin, or Comino, is native to the Mediterranean area. It is widely used when cooking with chiles. It can be purchased ground or as whole seeds.

Salsa for Scrambled Eggs

2 Tbsp. VEGETABLE OIL
1/2 cup BELL PEPPER, diced
1/4 cup ONION, diced
1 can (15 oz.) TOMATO SAUCE
1 Tbsp. LEMON JUICE
1 tsp. WORCESTERSHIRE SAUCE
1 tsp. ground RED CHILE POWDER

Sauté onion and bell pepper in oil until lightly browned. Add remaining ingredients, simmer 30 minutes.

Makes 2 cups.

Salsa for Shrimp

1/3 cup VEGETABLE OIL
3 cloves GARLIC, crushed
1 Tbsp. ground GINGER
2 Tbsp. LEMON JUICE
1 Tbsp. crushed RED CHILES

Sauté garlic in oil until lightly browned. Add other ingredients, heat completely. Pour over cooked shrimp.

Makes 1/2 cup.

To peel tomatoes, dip them into boiling water for a few seconds, then place under cool water. The skin peels off easily.

Salsa for Taco
or Tostada Topping

1 carton (2 cups) SOUR CREAM
1 Tbsp. fresh LIME JUICE
1 can (4 oz.) sliced JALAPEÑOS, drained
1 can (4 oz.) sliced BLACK OLIVES, drained

Stir all ingredients together. Serve in bowl to be passed at the table.

Makes 2 1/2 cups.

Salsa for Tostadas or Pizza

2 lbs. TOMATOES, diced
1/2 cup ONION, diced
1 BELL PEPPER, diced
2 Tbsp. canned or fresh JALAPEÑOS, diced
1/4 tsp. crushed RED PEPPERS
1/2 cup CIDER VINEGAR
1 tsp. SUGAR

Combine all ingredients and simmer until thickened, stirring frequently.

Makes 2 cups.

Salsa Fresca

4 med. TOMATOES, chopped
1 can (4 oz.) sliced BLACK OLIVES, drained
6 GREEN ONIONS, chopped with some tops
1 fresh ANAHEIM or NEW MEXICAN CHILE, seeded
    and diced
1 Tbsp. LIME JUICE
3 Tbsp. fresh CILANTRO, chopped
1/2 tsp. RED CHILE POWDER
1/4 tsp. ground CUMIN

Combine all ingredients and chill.

Makes 3 cups.

Salsa Fria for Hamburgers

This salsa makes a wonderful topping for hamburgers or hot dogs.

6 med. TOMATOES, peeled and finely diced
1/3 cup ONION, diced
1 can (4 oz.) diced GREEN CHILES
1/4 tsp. ground CUMIN
1/2 tsp. ground OREGANO
2 Tbsp. WINE VINEGAR
1 tsp. VEGETABLE OIL

Combine all ingredients and serve well-chilled.

Makes 2 cups.

Salsa Marinade for Vegetables

This salsa marinade is good for whatever fresh vegetables are available. Yellow and green squash (uncooked) combined with small whole mushrooms are delicious and look very attractive together.

2/3 cup RED WINE VINEGAR
1 cup VEGETABLE OIL
1 tsp. dried SWEET BASIL
1 Tbsp. LIME JUICE
1 dash TABASCO® sauce

Combine salsa ingredients and mix well. Marinate vegetables at least 2 hours or until well chilled. Serve vegetables on a leaf of lettuce.

Makes 2 cups.

Salsa over Black Beans

This salsa is traditionally served over black beans with a spoonful of sour cream on top.

2 lg. TOMATOES, diced
2 fresh JALAPEÑOS, seeded and diced
2 cloves GARLIC, pressed
1/4 cup GREEN ONIONS, cut in 1/2 inch pieces
1/4 cup fresh PARSLEY, chopped
1/4 cup fresh CILANTRO, chopped
SOUR CREAM, optional

Combine all ingredients and chill 4 hours, stirring occasionally to blend flavors.

Makes 3 cups.

Salsa Picante I

1 can (15 oz.) TOMATILLOS, drained, chopped
2 fresh JALAPEÑOS, seeded and diced
1 Tbsp. OLIVE OIL
1 Tbsp. WHITE WINE VINEGAR
2 tsp. SUGAR

Place all ingredients in blender and blend until smooth. May be served either cold or hot.

Makes 1 1/2 cups.

Salsa Picante II

1 cup OLIVE OIL
1 WHITE ONION, diced
1 cup RED WINE
1/4 cup GARLIC WINE VINEGAR
1 Tbsp. ground RED CHILE POWDER

Combine all ingredients and store until ready to use, either warm or chilled.

Makes 2 1/2 cups.

Cilantro, also known as Chinese Parsley, is sold in most markets and is the most widely used seasoning in salsas.

Salsa por Chicken or Turkey Enchiladas and Burritos

1 can (10 1/2 oz.) CHICKEN BROTH
1 1/4 cups WATER
1/2 cup VEGETABLE OIL
1/2 cup FLOUR
1 lg. can (15 oz.) TOMATO SAUCE
1/8 tsp. GARLIC POWDER
2 tsp. POULTRY SEASONING
2 Tbsp. ground RED CHILE POWDER
1 tsp. ground CUMIN

Mix broth and water to make 2 cups. Heat oil, gradually stirring in flour, blending until all the flour is absorbed. Slowly add broth and water mixture, stirring constantly until thickened. Add remaining ingredients slowly and simmer until entire mixture is slightly thickened.

Makes 4 cups.

Salsa por Chimichangas

1/3 cup VEGETABLE OIL
1 med. ONION, minced
2 cloves GARLIC, minced
1 can (15 oz.) TOMATOES, chunk style, drained
1 Tbsp. CHILE POWDER
1 tsp. ground CUMIN
1 can (4 oz.) diced GREEN CHILES

Heat oil, sauté onions and garlic until onions become limp. Add remaining ingredients and simmer slowly 5 minutes.

Makes 3 cups.

Salsa por Enchiladas

2 Tbsp. VEGETABLE OIL
2 Tbsp. FLOUR
1 1/2 cups WATER
1 can (8 oz.) TOMATO SAUCE
1/4 tsp. ground OREGANO
1/8 tsp. ground CUMIN
3 cloves GARLIC, crushed
2 Tbsp. package RED CHILE POWDER (not chili
powder, which contains other spices)

Heat oil, blend in flour, stir with whisk until all flour is absorbed. Stir in water, then tomato sauce and thicken, cooking slowly and stirring constantly. Add everything else and simmer 10 minutes.

Makes 2 1/2 cups.

Salsa por Scallops

1 lg. can TOMATOES, drained and chopped
1/2 cup ONION, chopped
1/2 tsp. GARLIC SALT
1/2 Tbsp. OLIVE OIL
1 tsp. ground CINNAMON
1 can (4 oz.) sliced JALAPEÑOS, with 1/2 of the
juice from can

Combine the ingredients and simmer slowly while cooking scallops. When scallops are cooked, arrange them on a bed of rice and cover with salsa. Serve extra salsa as gravy.

Makes 4 cups.

Salsa Roja I

3 TOMATOES
2 sm. fresh HOT CHILES
2 tsp. VEGETABLE OIL
2 cloves GARLIC

Place all ingredients in blender or food processor until smooth. Heat over medium heat.

Makes 1 cup.

Salsa Roja II

To try a salsa made from dried chiles, this is one that complements many dishes. The Ancho chile is one of Mexico's favorites.

1 package (4 oz.) dried ANCHO CHILES
2 Tbsp. VEGETABLE OIL
1 lg. ONION, chopped
3 cups VEGETABLE BROTH, canned, low sodium
1/2 tsp. ground CUMIN
1/2 tsp. ground OREGANO

Clean chiles carefully to remove any bits on the outside of the pod. A pastry brush works well for this. Roast chiles according to instructions in Chapter Two.

Sauté onions in oil until translucent, add broth, cumin and oregano. Cook over medium heat until chiles feel soft when pierced with a fork. Let mixture cool, put through food processor or blender.

Makes 3 cups.

Salsa Sandwich Spread

2 packages (3 oz.) CREAM CHEESE WITH CHIVES
1 package (3 oz.) CREAM CHEESE WITH PIMENTOS
1 can (7 oz.) diced GREEN CHILES, undrained

Soften cream cheeses, stir in chiles. Spread over deli sliced ham and roll up ham slices. Serve chilled.

Makes 1 1/4 cups.

Salsa Verde

1 can (15 oz.) TOMATILLOS, drained
2 JALAPEÑOS, seeded
1/3 cup ONION, chopped
1 tsp. dried CILANTRO
2 Tbsp. VEGETABLE OIL

Combine tomatillos, jalapenos, onion and cilantro in blender. Blend until smooth. Heat oil in small frying pan, add blender mixture and sauté lightly.

Makes 2 cups.

Chiles grown at home are considered perennials in warm climates and annuals in colder ones.

Salsa Verde con Carne

1 lb. lean GROUND BEEF
1/2 cup ONION diced
2 cloves GARLIC, minced
1 can (7 oz.) diced GREEN CHILES, undrained

Brown beef, onion and garlic until beef is cooked. Drain any fat. Return to pan and add chiles. Keep hot until served.

Makes 2 cups.

Salsa Vino

This salsa is delicious served with lamb chops and as a marinade for Leg of Lamb or Crown Roast of Lamb.

1 1/2 cups WHITE WINE
3 Tbsp. WHITE SUGAR
1/2 cup dried MINT LEAVES
1/2 cup dried CILANTRO

Mix wine and sugar and boil gently over medium heat until sugar is dissolved. Let cool slightly, stir in mint and cilantro. Let stand 1 hour to blend flavors.

Makes 1 1/2 cups.

Salsa with Bourbon

This salsa is particularly delicious served with barbecued meats. Mix leftover salsa with 8 oz. cream cheese and use as spread for chips.

2 Tbsp. VEGETABLE OIL
1 sm. ONION, minced
2 cloves GARLIC, pressed
1/2 cup CHILI SAUCE, from bottle
1 can (4 oz.) sliced JALAPEÑOS, with juice
1/2 cup light BROWN SUGAR
1/2 cup BOURBON
2 tsp. WORCESTERSHIRE SAUCE
2 tsp. dried LEMON PEEL

Mix all ingredients well and chill several hours or overnight.

Makes 2 cups.

Seafood Salsa

3 TOMATOES, chopped
1/4 cup ONION, diced
1 BELL PEPPER, diced, any color or 1 cup diced mixed frozen BELL PEPPER
1 tsp. fresh DILL or 1 tsp. dried DILL SEED
1 tsp. dried BASIL
3 Tbsp. LIME JUICE
2 Tbsp. OLIVE OIL
1 tsp. JALAPEÑO, diced
1 Tbsp. dried PARSLEY FLAKES

Mix well and refrigerate for several hours. Serve with seafood or fish.

Makes 2 cups.

Serrano Salsa

2 SERRANO CHILES, seeded and diced
2 TOMATOES, diced
1 can (8 oz.) TOMATO SAUCE
1/4 tsp. GARLIC SALT
1/4 cup WATER
1 tsp. dried OREGANO

Blend all ingredients on medium speed in blender. Let stand several hours.

Makes 1 1/2 cups.

Steak Salsa

3 JALAPEÑOS, seeded and diced
3 cloves GARLIC, crushed
1/3 cup ONION, diced
1 tsp. dried OREGANO or 2 tsp. fresh OREGANO
    leaves, chopped
1/2 tsp. cracked BLACK PEPPER
1/2 cup OLIVE OIL
1/2 RED WINE
1 Tbsp. LIME JUICE

Mix all ingredients and store in glass jar in refrigerator 24 hours. Serve in small individual bowls with steaks.

Makes 2 cups.

Sunflower Salsa

This unusual salsa is especially good served with roast pork or chicken.

1 cup SUNFLOWER SEEDS, shelled
1 Tbsp. OIL
1/4 tsp. CLOVES
1/2 tsp. CINNAMON
2 tsp. ground CHILI POWDER
1 tsp. COCOA
Sprinkle of GARLIC SALT
1 Tbsp. WHITE WINE
1 cup WATER or STOCK

Sauté seeds in oil over medium heat until lightly toasted. Combine toasted seeds, cloves, cinnamon, chili powder, cocoa, garlic salt, wine and 1/2 cup of water or stock in blender. Blend until smooth. Simmer mixture over medium heat, using remaining water or stock until slightly thickened.

Makes 1 1/2 cups.

Bell peppers got their name because they are shaped like a bell.

Super Duper Salsa

This salsa is very versatile and freezes without losing its rich flavor.

1 Tbsp. VEGETABLE OIL
1 med. ONION, diced
4 med. TOMATOES, diced
1 can (15 oz.) TOMATO SAUCE
3 JALAPEÑOS, seeded and diced
1 BELL PEPPER, seeded and diced
1 Tbsp. dried CILANTRO, crushed
1 Tbsp. WHITE VINEGAR

Simmer together oil, onion, tomatoes, tomato sauce, jalapeno, bell pepper and cilantro for 1 hour. Remove from heat and stir in the vinegar.

Let salsa cool before serving.

Makes 2 1/2 cups.

Super Salsa

4 lg. TOMATOES, chopped
1/2 cup ONION, chopped
3 ANAHEIM or other large GREEN CHILES, roasted,
    peeled, seeded and diced
3 JALAPEÑOS, seeded and diced
1/3 cup fresh CILANTRO, chopped
2 Tbsp. OIL
2 Tbsp. LIME JUICE
1/4 tsp. ground CLOVES
1/2 tsp. ground CUMIN (COMINO)

Combine all ingredients and let rest at room temperature for 1 hour. Super Salsa is wonderful served over foods or as a dip.

Makes 2 cups.

Chiles are members of the Capsicum
family, which also includes their milder
cousins known as peppers.

Superior Salsa

The mining town of Superior, Arizona, used to be difficult to get to on an old mountain road so it was important to stock up on canned products.

2 Tbsp. OIL (olive or vegetable)
2 cloves GARLIC, crushed
2 Tbsp. FLOUR
2 cups BOUILLON
1 can (15 oz.) tomatoes, drained
1 can (4 oz.) diced GREEN CHILES

Sauté crushed garlic in oil until lightly browned. Stir in flour until all flour is absorbed. Gradually stir in bouillon until salsa is smooth and thickened. Add tomatoes and chilis and simmer 10 minutes.

Makes 4 cups.

Sweet Spicy Salsa I

This salsa works well with any dish where a hint of sweet, yet pungent, flavor is desired. It can be refrigerated for up to 2 weeks and freezes well so make a large batch and have it handy in the freezer.

2 med. ONIONS, chopped
2 cloves GARLIC, crushed
2 Tbsp. BUTTER
1 can (15 oz.) TOMATO SAUCE
1 can (8 oz.) TOMATO SAUCE
1/2 cup BROWN SUGAR
1 Tbsp. CHILI POWDER
1/2 tsp. INSTANT COFFEE
1/2 tsp. DRY MUSTARD
1/4 tsp. TABASCO SAUCE
1/4 tsp. SMOKE
2 CHICKEN BOUILLON CUBES
1/2 cup LIME JUICE

Sauté onion and garlic in butter until onion is soft. Add all other ingredients, simmer slowly for 1 hour. Serve warm or chilled.

Makes 3 cups.

CAPSAICIN is a reddish brown, hot peppery liquid known chemically as $C_{18}H_{27}O_3N$. The liquid is frequently used in flavoring pickles and vinegar.

Sweet Spicy Salsa II

6 med. TOMATOES, chopped
2 med. WHITE ONIONS, chopped
1 BELL PEPPER, any color or mixed colors, chopped
1/4 cup DARK BROWN SUGAR
2 Tbsp. WHITE VINEGAR
2 sm. CHILES, seeded and diced or 1 can (4 oz.) diced
    GREEN CHILES
1/2 tsp. ground CINNAMON
1/2 tsp. ALLSPICE
1/8 tsp. ground CLOVES

Combine all ingredients and simmer for 1 hour uncovered. Remove from heat. Wonderful served with baked ham.

Makes 2 cups.

Swordfish Salsa

The more salsas one creates, the more they become associated with a favorite dish. This salsa makes grilled swordfish a very special treat.

2/3 cups OLIVE OIL
1 bunch (8-10) GREEN ONIONS, minced with some
    tops
1/3 cup LIME JUICE
1 Tbsp. canned, sliced JALAPEÑOS with 1 tsp. juice
    from can
1/2 bunch fresh CILANTRO, minced
Freshly cracked LEMON PEPPER to taste

Combine all ingredients and chill several hours.

Makes 1 1/3 cups.

Tequila Salsa

This salsa is particularly good with turkey or chicken. It can be used as a salsa or as a marinade.

1/2 cup OLIVE OIL
1/2 cup LIME JUICE
1/2 cup TEQUILA
2 Tbsp. TRIPLE SEC
1 can (4 oz.) diced GREEN CHILES, undrained

Combine all ingredients. If using as a salsa, serve chilled.

Makes 2 cups.

Tomatillo Salsa I

1 lb. TOMATILLO, peeled, chopped
1/2 cup JALAPEÑO, diced
1/2 cup BEEF BOUILLON
1/2 cup LIME JUICE
1 Tbsp. dried CILANTRO

Simmer all ingredients together for 20 minutes. Serve warm over beef.

Makes 2 cups.

Tomatillo Salsa II

This makes a tangy tomatillo salsa.

1 can (13 oz.) TOMATILLOS, drained and diced
2 JALAPEÑO CHILES, seeded and diced, or 1 can
    (4 oz.) diced JALAPEÑOS
1/4 cup ONION, minced
1/2 tsp. dried LEMON PEEL
1/2 tsp. WHITE SUGAR
1 Tbsp. dried CILANTRO, crushed

Combine all ingredients and refrigerate several hours or overnight.

Makes 1 1/2 cups.

Tomatillo Salsa III

1/2 lb. TOMATILLOS, fresh or canned (if canned, drain)
1/4 cup ONION, diced
2 cloves GARLIC, pressed
1 tsp. OIL (not olive)
2 JALAPEÑOS, seeded and diced

Heat oil and sauté the tomatillos, onions, garlic and jalapeños for 3 minutes until tomatillos are soft.

Makes 1 cup.

Wine Salsa for Baked Ham

1 1/2 cups PORT
1/2 cup SUGAR (white or light brown)
1/2 tsp. LEMON PEEL
1/2 tsp. ORANGE PEEL
1 JALAPEÑO CHILE, minced

Heat all ingredients, simmering gently. Serve in a gravy boat.

Makes 1 1/2 cups.

Yellow Fruit Salsa

A tangy salsa for delicately flavored fish.

1 can (15 oz.) TOMATOES, drained
1 can (8 1/4 oz.) PINEAPPLE chunks, drained
1 cup PAPAYA, if available, peeled and diced
1 JALAPEÑO, seeded and diced
2 Tbsp. LIME JUICE

Mix all ingredients and let stand covered in refrigerator for several hours.

Makes 3 cups.

Yellow Salsa

5 YELLOW WAX CHILES
1 JALAPEÑO
1 lg. can STEWED TOMATOES
1 GREEN ONION, minced
1/4 tsp. each OREGANO, GARLIC POWDER and SALT

Cook chiles, peel and remove seeds. Place roasted and peeled chiles and all other ingredients in blender. Blend until smooth.

Makes 2 cups.

Yellow Squash Salsa

2 YELLOW CROOKNECK SQUASH, uncooked, diced
1/4 cup ONION, diced
1/4 cup BELL PEPPER, any color, diced
1 can (15 oz.) TOMATOES AND GREEN CHILES,
    drained, chopped
1 JALAPEÑO, seeded and diced
1/4 tsp. ground CUMIN

Combine all ingredients and chill well.

Makes 2 cups.

CHAPTER V

Fruits and Salads

Southwestern markets blossom with fruits and vegetables that stir the imagination. Even though many of the regional cuisines in the southwest are served with fruits and vegetables (especially lettuce and tomatoes) spectacular salads (Ensaladas) are a specialty of southwestern chefs.

Not all salads are served with dressing. Fresh lime juice makes an ideal dressing for some salads. Many salsas from the appetizers chapter make a wonderful topping for salads, too.

Avocado Salsa

2 lg. ripe AVOCADOS
1 lg. TOMATO, chopped
1 Tbsp. diced GREEN CHILES
1 Tbsp. ONION, diced
1 Tbsp. CILANTRO, chopped
2 Tbsp. WINE (not red)

Mash avocados, stir in remaining ingredients. Serve over crisp lettuce as salad dressing.

Makes 1 1/2 cups.

Avocado Salsa for Salads

1 lg. AVOCADO, diced
1/2 cup SOUR CREAM
1 clove GARLIC, crushed
1 tsp. dried CILANTRO
1 tsp. TABASCO® or other hot sauce
2 Tbsp. LIME JUICE

Combine all ingredients in blender. Serve well chilled over salad.

Makes 1 1/2 cups.

Chile Butter

1 can (4 oz.) diced GREEN CHILES
1 lb. BUTTER, softened
Sprinkle of GARLIC POWDER
1/4 cup fresh CILANTRO, chopped
**   or 2 Tbsp. dried CILANTRO**
1 tsp. LIME JUICE

Blend all ingredients well. This butter has unlimited uses. It is wonderful for scrambling eggs and as a spread for rolls and crackers.

Chile butter keeps well in the refrigerator. If freezing is desired, use dried cilantro.

Makes 1 1/4 lbs.

Easy Salsa
for Mixed Salad Greens

1 cup OLIVE OIL
3 tsp. DIJON MUSTARD
4 Tbsp. WINE VINEGAR
1/4 tsp. SALT
1/4 tsp. CRACKED PEPPER

Combine all ingredients and beat well with wire wisk. Salsa will thicken slightly when beaten. Toss with chilled greens.

Makes 1 1/2 cups.

Ensalada Salsa

4 Tbsp. OLIVE OIL
1 Tbsp. BASIL VINEGAR
1 Tbsp. TABASCO® SAUCE
1/2 tsp. dried CILANTRO (Coriander Leaf)
1/8 tsp. freshly cracked BLACK PEPPER

This basic salad salsa can be made several hours before serving. Make any quantity desired and store in glass jar in refrigerator.

Makes 1/2 cup.

Guacamole Salsa for Salads

1 carton SOUR CREAM
2 AVOCADOS, mashed
2 Tbsp. LIME JUICE
1 Tbsp. canned sliced JALAPEÑOS with
1 tsp. juice from can

Combine all the ingredients well and prepare salad at once.

Makes 1 1/2 cups.

Salad Salsa

This basic salad salsa stores well in jars in the refrigerator.

2 cups VEGETABLE OIL
1 ONION, minced
1/2 cup WHITE WINE VINEGAR
1/2 cup SUGAR
2 Tbsp. dried CILANTRO
2 Tbsp. TABASCO® SAUCE or other liquid RED
**   PEPPER SAUCE.**

Mix all ingredients and chill well.

Makes 2 1/2 cups.

Salsa con Hierbas

(Salsa with Herbs)

A wonderful salsa for mixed green salads. This stores well in a glass jar in the refrigerator so keep plenty on hand.

1 cup OLIVE OIL
2 Tbsp. LIME JUICE
3 Tbsp. BASIL VINEGAR
1 tsp. dried OREGANO
1/4 tsp. GARLIC SALT
1/4 tsp. PEPPER
1 jar (3 oz.) diced PIMENTOS
2 shakes dried LEMON PEEL
1 tsp. SUGAR

Blend all ingredients in blender. Store in refrigerator.

Makes 1 1/2 cups.

Salsa for Caesar Salad

History says that the Caesar salad originated on the west coast of Mexico. Whatever its true origin, there is no doubt it is one of the world's favorite salads. Whether the salad is served plain or with chicken or lobster, this salsa is wonderful.

2 cups OLIVE OIL
8 cloves GARLIC, crushed
1 can (4 oz.) diced GREEN CHILES
2 Tbsp. LIME JUICE
2 Tbsp. WHITE VINEGAR
1 1/2 Tbsp. DIJON MUSTARD

Combine all ingredients and blend well with wire whisk. Serve at once.

Makes 2 1/2 cups.

Cold Pinto Bean Salad

Chill fresh or canned (well rinsed and drained) pinto or other beans, or a combination, for several hours. Just before serving, add 1/2 cup diced onion and 1/4 cup diced jalapeño to beans. Toss well with following salsa.

2/3 cup OLIVE OIL
4 Tbsp. WHITE WINE VINEGAR
1/8 tsp. fresh cracked LEMON PEPPER
1/8 tsp. ALLSPICE

Combine all ingredients and blend well with wire whisk.

Makes 1 cup.

Salsa for Fruit Salad

2 Tbsp. OLIVE OIL
2 Tbsp. VINEGAR
1/2 cup SOUR CREAM
1 tsp. LEMON JUICE
1 tsp. SUGAR
1/2 tsp. ground CUMIN
2 Tbsp. MINT LEAVES, chopped
2 Tbsp. fresh CILANTRO, chopped

Combine all ingredients and mix very well. Chill well.

Makes 1 1/4 cups.

Salsa for Salad Greens

1/4 cup prepared SALSA
1/4 cup RED WINE VINEGAR
1/3 cup OLIVE OIL
3 Tbsp. LIME JUICE
2 tsp. dried CILANTRO
1/2 tsp. CUMIN

Combine the ingredients and chill. Toss with salad greens.

Makes 2 cups.

Salsa for Vegetable Salads I

A wonderful salsa for vegetable salads or as a dip for fresh vegetables.

1/2 cup OLIVE OIL
3 Tbsp. LIME or LEMON JUICE
3 Tbsp. BASIL VINEGAR
3 Tbsp. canned GREEN CHILES, diced
1/2 tsp. SUGAR
1/4 tsp. each SALT and PEPPER
1/2 cup PIMENTO, diced

Combine all ingredients and blend well.

Makes 1 1/2 cups.

Salsa for Vegetable Salads II

1/2 cup VEGETABLE OIL
1/4 cup RED WINE VINEGAR
1 clove GARLIC, crushed
1/4 tsp. dried OREGANO
1/4 tsp. PARSLEY FLAKES

Combine all ingredients and mix well. Refrigerate all day or overnight. Toss with mixed vegetables.

Makes 1 cup.

Salsa for Watercress Salad

Prepare individual salad bowls of desired amounts of watercress, fresh mushrooms and finely sliced red onions.

OLIVE OIL
BALSAMIC VINEGAR
SUGAR

Depending upon the number of salads, mix olive oil, vinegar and sugar, using equal amounts of each.

CATSUP
TABASCO®

Mix together enough catsup and tabasco, using equal amounts of each, to equal the amount used of the other three ingredients. Combine all together and serve well chilled over the salad mixture.

Salsa Mango

1 MANGO, peeled and diced
2 Tbsp. GREEN ONIONS, diced
2 Tbsp. BELL PEPPER, any color, diced
2 Tbsp. WINE VINEGAR
2 Tbsp. fresh CILANTRO or PARSLEY, chopped
1 lg. ripe AVOCADO, chopped

Mix all ingredients except avocado and refrigerate several hours. When ready to serve, add avocado. Serve over mixed greens as a salad dressing or as a garnish with fish or poultry.

Makes 1 cup.

Warm Salsa for Spinach Salad

1/2 cup OLIVE OIL
2 cloves GARLIC, crushed
2 Tbsp. GARLIC WINE VINEGAR
1 can (7 oz.) diced GREEN CHILES
1/2 cup crisp BACON, diced
1 tsp. dried CILANTRO, crushed

Combine all ingredients. Just before serving, warm 10 seconds on full power in microwave.

Makes 1 cup.

CHAPTER VI

Dessert Salsa

Some of the most delicious of all salsas are those that end the meal. Mexican chocolate is one of the world's best and the variety of chocolate salsas is endless. There are as many chocolate salsas as there are creative minds.

Salsas using citrus and other fruits are also very popular. In most warm climates, a large variety of fresh citrus and fruits are available all year. Salsa is usually served with all desserts.

Banana Salsa

2 BANANAS
1/4 cup SUGAR
1/2 cup CREAM
1 tsp. VANILLA
1 Tbsp. RUM

Mash bananas, add remaining ingredients and stir well. Serve over cake.

Makes 1 1/2 cups.

Butterscotch Salsa

Perfect for vanilla ice cream!

1/2 cup SUGAR
1/2 cup BROWN SUGAR
1 cup CORN SYRUP
3 Tbsp. BUTTER
2/3 cup CREAM
2 tsp. VANILLA

Mix all ingredients, bring to a boil, simmer gently for 5 minutes. Remove from heat and stir in vanilla. Cool and refrigerate.

Makes 2 cups.

Candied Salsa for Fruit Desserts

2 Tbsp. BUTTER
1/3 cup BROWN SUGAR
2 tsp. ORANGE RIND
1 cup ORANGE JUICE
1/8 tsp. CINNAMON
1/4 tsp. NUTMEG

Melt butter over medium heat. Add remaining ingredients. Reduce heat, stirring constantly until sugar melts. Serve at once. This can be made in advance and heated in the microwave.

Makes 1 cup.

Champagne Salsa

An elegant salsa sometimes served traditionally on special holidays.

1 cup ORANGE JUICE
1 Tbsp. CORNSTARCH
2 Tbsp. light BROWN SUGAR
1 cup sliced STRAWBERRIES
1 cup CHAMPAGNE

Mix orange juice and cornstarch and bring to a boil. Simmer 1-2 minutes. Remove from heat while still simmering, stir in brown sugar, strawberries and champagne.

Makes 2 1/2 cups.

Chocolate Salsa I

8 oz. bittersweet CHOCOLATE
3 Tbsp. BUTTER
1/4 cup MILK
1/2 cup CREAM
1/2 cup COCOA
1/3 cup CORN SYRUP

Combine all ingredients, heat slowly, stirring constantly until glossy.

Makes 1 1/2 cups.

Chocolate Salsa II

1/2 cup COCOA
1 cup MILK
1 cup SUGAR
1 tsp. CORNSTARCH
1 cup CREAM
1 Tbsp. BUTTER
1 Tbsp. any flavor LIQUEUR

Stir cocoa, milk, sugar, cornstarch and cream together in pan. Cook over medium heat until thickened. Remove from heat, add liqueur and butter.

Makes 2 cups.

Chocolate Salsa III

1/2 cup COCOA
2 Tbsp. SUGAR
1 Tbsp. CORNSTARCH
1/3 cup light CORN SYRUP
1/2 cup MILK
2 Tbsp. KAHLUA®

Mix cocoa, sugar, cornstarch, corn syrup and milk. Boil gently over medium heat, stirring constantly. Let cool slightly, add kahlua.

Makes 1 cup.

Chocolate Salsa IV

1/2 cup COCOA
1 cup CORN SYRUP
1 cup SUGAR
2 Tbsp. BUTTER
2/3 cup CREAM
1 1/2 tsp. VANILLA

Mix cocoa, syrup, sugar, butter and cream and bring to a boil. Reduce heat and simmer 5 minutes. Remove from heat, cool 5 minutes, stir in vanilla.

Makes 2 1/2 cups.

Chocolate Salsa V

12 oz. CHOCOLATE
1 lb. BUTTER
1 cup very strong COFFEE, any flavor
2 tsp. VANILLA

Heat chocolate and coffee together with butter until all the butter is melted. Remove from heat. Add vanilla. This sauce is especially good with ice cream.

Makes 1 1/2 cups.

Chocolate Salsa VI

1/3 cup COCOA
1 Tbsp. SUGAR
1/3 cup MILK
1 Tbsp. CORNSTARCH
1/3 cup CORN SYRUP
1 tsp. CORN OIL
1 tsp. COFFEE LIQUEUR

Mix cocoa, sugar, milk, cornstarch and syrup in pan. Boil over medium heat, stirring constantly. Remove from heat, stir in oil and liqueur.

Makes 1 cup.

Coffee Salsa

Marvelous over coffee or butter pecan ice cream.

1/2 cup BUTTER
8 oz. unsweetened CHOCOLATE
1/4 cup SUGAR
1/4 cup INSTANT COFFEE
1/4 cup GRAND MARNIER®

Combine butter, chocolate and sugar over low heat stirring constantly until melted. Remove from heat, stir in the coffee and Grand Marnier.

Makes 1 1/2 cups.

Drunken Salsa

This is wonderful served with pecan pie.

1/2 cup SUGAR
1/2 cup BROWN SUGAR
1/2 cup WATER
2 Tbsp. ORANGE JUICE
1 cup CREAM
1/2 cup BOURBON

Combine sugar, brown sugar, water and orange juice. Bring to boil and simmer until the sugar is dissolved. Remove from heat, stir in cream, slowly, and bourbon.

Makes 2 cups.

Lemon Salsa

1/4 cup BUTTER
1 cup SUGAR
Juice of one LEMON
1 tsp. grated LEMON RIND
2 Tbsp. WATER

Combine all ingredients and bring slowly to a boil, stirring briskly. Boil 30 seconds. Serve over cake.

Note: When grating lemon rind, be careful to use only the colored portion of the rind.

Makes 3/4 cup.

Mexican Coffee

4 cups WATER
1/3 cup DARK BROWN SUGAR
1/2 cup INSTANT COFFEE
4 CINNAMON STICKS

Combine water and sugar, bring to a boil, stirring until sugar is dissolved. Reduce heat and stir in coffee, simmer two minutes. Pour into individual mugs, add a cinnamon stick to each mug. Stir coffee with stick.

Makes 4 cups.

Mexican Hot Cocoa

1/4 cup COCOA
1/4 cup SUGAR
3/4 tsp. CINNAMON
1 qt. WHOLE MILK
1/3 cup HEAVY CREAM
1 tsp. VANILLA

Combine cocoa, sugar and cinnamon. Set aside. Heat 1 cup of milk until bubbly, stir in cocoa mixture, mix with wisk until smooth. Gradually stir in remaining milk so slow boiling continues. Remove from heat, stir in cream and vanilla. Mix well.

Makes 5 cups.

Orange Peach Salsa

This salsa is also used as a salsa for baked ham.

1 cup PEACH PRESERVES
1/2 cup ORANGE JUICE
3 Tbsp. GRAND MARNIER®

Heat preserves and juice, stirring constantly until preserves are melted. Cool slightly and stir in Grand Marnier.

Makes 1 cup.

Orange Salsa

Wonderful served with a mixed fruit compote.

1/4 cup ORANGE JUICE
3 cups ORANGE MARMALADE
1 1/2 Tbsp. LEMON JUICE
3 Tbsp. BUTTER
1/2 cup ORANGE LIQUEUR

Combine all ingredients and simmer for 15 minutes. Serve warm over cake or ice cream.

Makes 2 cups.

Peach Salsa

1 lb. PEACHES, frozen or fresh
3/4 cup SUGAR
3/4 cup ORANGE JUICE
1/2 cup white or blush WINE
3 tsp. VANILLA

Combine peaches, sugar and orange juice and bring to a boil over medium heat. Cook 10 minutes, adding wine the last 2 minutes. Remove from heat. Stir in vanilla.

Makes 3 cups.

Pineapple Dessert Salsa

1 lg. can crushed PINEAPPLE, do not drain
3 Tbsp. SUGAR
2 Tbsp. CORNSTARCH

Mix sugar and cornstarch, add pineapple and cook over medium heat until bubbly. Serve over pound cake.

Makes 1 1/2 cups.

Raisin and Rum Salsa

1 cup RAISINS
2 cups SUGAR
2 tsp. CORNSTARCH
2 tsp. LEMON JUICE
3 Tbsp. BUTTER
1/2 cup PECANS, chopped
1/2 cup DARK RUM

Simmer raisins in 1 1/2 cups water 30 minutes. Stir in sugar and cornstarch, simmer 5 more minutes. Remove from heat, stir in butter. When butter melts, stir in lemon juice, pecans and rum. Cover and refrigerate.

Makes 3 cups.

Raspberry Salsa

Wonderful over chocolate ice cream.

2 cups RASPBERRIES, frozen or fresh
3 Tbsp. SUGAR
1 Tbsp. CORNSTARCH, dissolved in 2 Tbsp. WATER
3 Tbsp. RASPBERRY LIQUEUR

Heat raspberries and sugar to boiling. Add cornstarch mixture, stirring well. Remove from heat and stir in liqueur.

Makes 1 1/2 cups.

Rum Salsa

Serve this salsa warm over cake. Very good with chocolate cake.

1 1/3 cups DARK BROWN SUGAR
1/2 cup WATER
3/4 cup light CORN SYRUP
3 Tbsp. BUTTER
1/3 cup DARK RUM

Combine all except rum and cook over medium heat until mixture comes to a boil. Boil softly 1 minute. Remove from heat and cool to room temperature. Stir in rum.

Makes 2 cups.

Rum Salsa for Spice Cake

1/2 cup BUTTER
1 cup SUGAR
1 cup hot WATER
1 EGG
1/3 cup DARK RUM

Cream butter and sugar together. Add hot water gradually until about the consistency of honey. Add the hot mixture gradually to the beaten egg, beating after each addition. Add rum. Serve hot over spice cake.

Makes 2 cups.

Strawberry Salsa

1 lb. STRAWBERRIES, frozen or fresh
1/2 cup SUGAR
1/2 cup CREAM
1/2 cup ORANGE FLAVORED LIQUEUR

Place all ingredients in blender and mix on medium speed. Wonderful served over vanilla ice cream.

Makes 2 cups.

Wine Salsa for Fruit

1 cup SUGAR
1 cup WINE (not red)
1/2 cup WATER
1 Tbsp. ORANGE JUICE
2 tsp. GINGER

Simmer sugar, water, orange juice and ginger until sugar is dissolved. Remove from heat, stir in wine. Good over all fruit.

Makes 2 cups.

Wine Salsa for Fruitcake

This basic salsa can be made with different kinds of wine depending upon its intended use. This recipe can be made with wine or liqueur.

1 cup SWEET WINE
1 cup WATER
1 1/2 cup BROWN SUGAR
1/2 tsp. ground CINNAMON
1/4 tsp. dried ORANGE PEEL

Combine all ingredients and boil until just beginning to thicken. Serve warm. Keep unused salsa refrigerated.

Makes 2 1/2 cups.

CHAPTER VII

Storing and Freezing Salsa

There is no substitute for fresh salsa but to preserve leftovers or salsa for gifts, camping trips or just to have a ready supply, here are some ideas.

Salsa can be processed for canning just like any other relish-type mixture. Always use glass jars when processing salsa. They make welcome gifts.

Salsa can be frozen. When preparing salsa for the freezer, omit fresh cilantro, using either the dried form, or adding fresh after thawing. Freezing is great for picnics or long car trips. Freeze salsa in sealer bags in amounts for specific needs, pack the frozen bags in your picnic hamper. When you arrive, your salsa is ready to eat.

Another choice for saving uneaten fresh salsa is to mix it with a commercially prepared salsa, which is designed to last a long time in the refrigerator. But remember, the fresh salsa contains no preservatives; therefore, when mixing the two, be aware that you no longer have an "indefinite" salsa.

Leftover salsa mixed with cottage cheese makes a wonderful dip or salad. If salsa is watery, drain in colander before adding to cottage cheese. If the mixture is still too watery, add softened cream cheese, either the plain variety or any of the flavored ones.

Salsa also makes a wonderful topping for baked dishes such as meatloaf or chicken.

Freezing chiles with the charred skins intact and double-wrapped in freezer bags helps preserve their flavor.

If the power to your freezer is interrupted, do not open the door any more than necessary. Food in a full freezer will remain frozen for up to two full days. Food in a half-filled freezer will remain frozen for up to one full day. Dry ice can be used to help prevent frozen foods from spoiling.

Making your own
Red Chile Powder

Note: Wear protective gloves when handling chiles.

25 DRIED RED CHILES

Rinse chiles and pat dry. Bake in single layer in 400 degree oven, being careful not to burn. Remove from oven when skin is stiff. Let cool.

Remove stems and seeds along with veins. Place in blender at high speed and grind to powder.

Store powder in glass jars in freezer.

Makes 1 cup powder.

Glossary of Southwestern Cuisine

This glossary describes some of the most commonly used terms and ingredients in southwestern cuisine. Where helpful, the Spanish word is given in parentheses. Herbs and spices are described elsewhere in this book.

Buñuelos: Similar to a fritter and frequently used for dessert.

Burro, Burrito: Flour tortillas filled with a mixture of choice, folded or rolled and frequently topped with a variety of salsas and vegetables.

Beans (Frijoles): Along with corn, beans are one of the most important ingredients of southwestern cooking. There are many varieties but these are some of the most common.

> **Anasazi Beans:** One of the oldest Indian beans, dark red and white color.
>
> **Black Beans (Frijoles Negro):** Also called turtle beans, they are very dark purple.
>
> **Pinto Beans:** The most well known and common and a native of the southwestern United States. "Pinto" means painted and these beans are mottled pink and brown in color.
>
> **White Beans (Frijoles Blanco):** Also known as "Navy" beans, these beans are used throughout the United States.

Calabaza: A vegetable known as Mexican squash or pumpkin and interchangeable with zucchini in recipes.

Beer: Cervesa

Ceviche: Raw, cold and marinated fish or seafood.

Chayote: A pear-shaped, light green squash interchangeable with scalloped edge (Patty-Pan) squash.

Cheese: (Queso)

Chicken: (Pollo)

Chile con Queso: Chiles mixed with cheese, frequently served as an appetizer.

Chile Relleno: Chile filled with a stuffing.

Chorizo: A spicy sausage

Corn: (Maiz)

Cucumber: (Pepino)

Egg: (Huevo)

Empanada: A turnover, usually filled with a meat, vegetables or a sweet filling.

Enchilada: A tortilla, usually corn, filled with any combination and rolled or stacked in layers.

Enchilada, Flat: A thick, pancake-like masa mixture, deep fried and served with Salsa Roja.

Flan: A caramel custard dessert.

Fried: (Frito)

Guacamole: An avocado mixture.

Ice cream: (Helado)

Jalapeno: Medium sized, hot chiles

Jicama: A potato-like, vegetable frequently used in salads. Mild tasting.

Mango: A popular tropical fruit.

Masa: Corn flour that has been treated and is used to make tortillas, flat enchiladas and tamales.

Milk: (Leche)

Nachos: Tortilla chips topped with various mixtures and usually served as an appetizer.

Papaya: A popular tropical fruit.

Pine Nuts (piñons): A nut crop native to southwestern United States.

Pineapple: (Piña)

Quesadilla: A tortilla with a filling, folded over and fried or grilled.

Rice: (Arroz)

Salt: (Sal)

Sopaipilla: A deep-fried, puffy bread, frequently served as a dessert with honey or a sweet dessert salsa.

Taco: A tortilla, usually corn, that is folded in half, fried and filled.

Tamale: Masa filled with a choice of filling, wrapped in corn husks and steamed until cooked.

Tomatillo: A small, firm green tomato-like fruit that is covered with a papery husk. In addition to the tomato, the tomatillo is the most popular ingredient in southwestern salsas.

Tortilla: Either corn or flour, a thin pancake-like bread that is the basis of most southwestern dishes.

Tostada: A fried tortilla served flat and topped with a variety of mixtures.

Topopo: A fried tortilla, usually corn, and topped with salad ingredients—a Mexican salad.

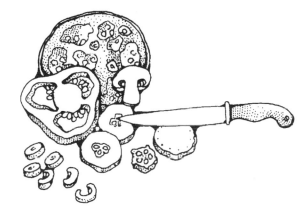

Salsa Serving Suggestions

— Beef —

— Poultry —

— Fish & Seafood —

— Vegetables & Eggs —

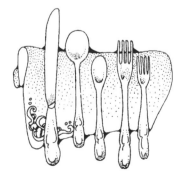

INDEX

T

Tequila   58, 85
Tequila Salsa   85
Tiger Salsa   28
Tomatillo Salsa   85, 86
Tomatillos   13, 33, 34, 39,
    51, 52, 62, 71, 75,
    85, 86
Tomato puree   60
Tomato sauce   26, 48, 59,
    61, 65, 67, 78, 83
Tomatoes   19-20, 22-28, 34-38,
    40-41, 43, 46, 49, 51, 53-57,
    60-62, 64, 66, 68-70, 72-74,
    77-78, 80-81, 84, 87-88, 90
Triple sec   85

V

V-8 Juice   66
Vegetable consommé   60
Vegetable Salsa   44

W

Warm Salsa for Spinach Salad   98
Watermelon   56

Whipping cream   55
White wine   76, 79
White wine vinegar   71
Wine   90, 112
**Wine Salsa for Baked
    Ham   87**
Wine Salsa for Fruit 112
**Wine Salsa for Fruit-
    cake   112**

Y

Yellow bell pepper   35
Yellow chiles   30
Yellow crookneck
    squash   88
Yellow Fruit Salsa   87
Yellow Salsa   88
Yellow squash   44
**Yellow Squash
    Salsa   88**
Yellow wax chiles   88

Z

Zucchini squash   44

More Cook Books by Golden West Publishers

Mexican Family Favorites Cook Book

More than 250 easy-to-follow homestyle recipes for tacos, tamales, menudo, enchiladas, burros, salsas, frijoles, chile rellenos, carne seca, guacamole, breads and sweet treats! By Maria Teresa Bermudez.

5 1/2 x 8 1/2—144 pages . . . $5.95

Mexican Desserts and Drinks

More than 200 recipes for Mexican festival desserts, custards, fruits, puddings, gelatins, cakes, pies, cookies, ice creams, sherbets and beverages, too! Just right for your sweet tooth! Olé!

5 1/2 x 8 1/2—144 pages . . . $6.95

Chili-Lovers' Cook Book

Chili cook-off prize winning recipes and regional favorites! Best of chili cookery, from mild to fiery, with and without beans. Plus taste-tempting foods made with chile peppers. By Al and Mildred Fischer. 150,000 copies in print!

5 1/2 x 8 1/2—128 pages . . . $5.95

Arizona Cook Book

A taste of the Old Southwest! Sizzling Indian fry bread, prickly pear marmalade, sourdough biscuits, refried beans, beef jerky and cactus candy. By Al and Mildred Fischer. More than 250,000 copies in print!

5 1/2 x 8 1/2—144 Pages . . . $5.95

New Mexico Cook Book

Authentic history and foods of New Mexico. Includes chapters on Indian heritage, chile as a way of life, Mesilla Valley, Santa Fe, Albuquerque, Taos and New Wave recipes. By Lynn Nusom, master chef.

5 1/2 x 8 1/2—144 pages . . . $5.95

Cowboy CartoonCookbook

Zesty western recipes, cowboy cartoons and anecdotes. Cowboy artist Jim Willoughby and his wife, Sue, combined their many talents to produce these palate-pleasing selections. Saddle up the stove, 'cause you'll be riding the range tonight! Yee-hah!

5 1/2 x 8 1/2—128 pages . . . $5.95

Christmas in Arizona

'Tis the season . . . celebrate Christmas in sunny Arizona. Read about the fascinating southwestern traditions and foods. Create a southwestern holiday spirit with this wonderful cookbook. By Lynn Nusom.

6 x 9—128 pages . . . $8.95

Christmas in New Mexico

Recipes, traditions and folklore for the Holiday Season—or all year long. Try *Three Kings Bread, Posole de Posada, Christmas Pumpkin Pie, Christmas Turkey with White Wine Basting Sauce*, and many more taste tempters! Makes an excellent gift! By Lynn Nusom.

6 x 9—144 pages . . . $8.95

More Cook Books by Golden West Publishers

Best Barbecue Recipes

A collection of more than 200 taste-tempting recipes. • Sauces • Rubs • Marinades • Mops • Ribs • Wild Game • Fish and Seafood • Pit barbecue and more! By Mildred Fischer.

5 1/2 x 8 1/2—144 pages . . . $5.95

California Favorites Cook Book

Over 400 Recipes!

Cooking adventures with avocados, citrus, dates, figs, nuts, raisins, Spanish and Mexican dishes, wines, salads and seafoods. By Al and Mildred Fischer.

5 1/2 x 8 1/2—144 pages . . . $5.95

Colorado Favorites Cook Book

Bring a taste of Colorado to your dinner table! Sample fishermen's fillets, gold miners' stews, Native American and Southwestern favorites, vegetarian feasts and skiers' hot toddies! Recipes, facts and folklore about Colorado.

5 1/2 x 8 1/2—128 pages . . . $5.95

The Joy of Muffins

The International Muffin Cook Book

Recipes for German Streusel, Finnish Cranberry, Italian Amaretto, Greek Baklava, Chinese Almond, Jamaican Banana, Swiss Fondue, microwave section and ten recipes for oat bran muffins . . . 150 recipes in all! By Genevieve Farrow and Diane Dreher.

5 1/2 x 8 1/2—120 pages . . . $5.95

ORDER BLANK

GOLDEN WEST ☼ PUBLISHERS

1-800-658-5830
(602) 265-4392
FAX 1-602-279-6901
4113 N. Longview • Phoenix, AZ 85014

Number of Copies	TITLE	Per Copy	AMOUNT
	Apple-Lovers' Cook Book	6.95	
	Arizona Cook Book	5.95	
	Best Barbecue Recipes	5.95	
	California Favorites Cook Book	5.95	
	Chili-Lovers' Cook Book	5.95	
	Christmas in Arizona Cook Book	8.95	
	Christmas in New Mexico Cook Book	8.95	
	Colorado Favorites Cook Book	5.95	
	Cowboy Cartoon Cook Book	5.95	
	Easy Recipes for Wild Game & Fish	6.95	
	Favorite Pumpkin Recipes	6.95	
	Joy of Muffins	5.95	
	Mexican Desserts & Drinks	6.95	
	Mexican Family Favorites Cook Book	5.95	
	New Mexico Cook Book	5.95	
	Pecan-Lovers' Cook Book	6.95	
	Salsa Lovers Cook Book	5.95	
	Add $2.00 to total order for shipping & handling		$2.00

☐ My Check or Money Order Enclosed. . . . . $_____

☐ MasterCard   ☐ VISA

Acct. No. _____   Exp. Date _____

Signature _____

Name _____   Telephone _____

Address _____

City/State/Zip _____

Call for FREE catalog

MasterCard and VISA Orders Accepted ($20 Minimum)

1/93

Salsa Ckbk

This order blank may be photo-copied.